Praise for *With Respect to the Japanese: Going to Work in Japan*

"I spent 20 years in Japan, but I can honestly say that *With Respect to the Japanese* opened my eyes to a new and more helpful understanding of the key values and assumptions underlying the way that Japanese think and interact. This new edition has even more practical advice and insights than the first, and I trust it will enlighten the many Westerners now working with Japanese companies in the same way that it did for me.
                    —**Ted Dale, president & Chief Creative Officer, Aperian Global**

"A beautifully balanced insider-outsider view of Japanese culture. If the reader observes and participates in Japanese business and culture as the authors suggest, they will no doubt succeed in whatever they intend to do in Japan."
        —**Kichiro Hayashi, PhD, professor emeritus, Aoyama Gakuin University, Tokyo, and former president of Japan Society of Multicultural Relations**

"Like gourmet chefs, John Condon and Tomoko Masumoto invite us to taste, smell, feel, and experience the rich, subtle, and complex aspects of the Japanese culture. Each course is brilliantly crafted and served, the rhythm flowing seamlessly between concepts, comparisons, examples, and applications. Reading this book makes me want to go to Japan . . . now!"
        —**Nagesh Rao, professor, Indian Institute of Management, Ahmedabad, India**

"A valuable book for those working in Japan for the first time, as well as for those who are in the position to teach or train newcomers to Japan . . . to understand what is expected at the Japanese workplace."
        —**Eriko Machi, professor, Reitaku University and president, SIETAR Japan**

"The authors' remarkable cross-cultural acumen shines in this practical, approachable guide to Japanese culture. Rich with illuminating examples, keen observations, and thoughtful explanations, *With Respect to the Japanese* is a superb handbook for Western professionals seeking to understand and appreciate the ways of their Japanese counterparts. Indeed, this insightful book provides readers with a template for approaching any new culture with self-awareness and sensitivity."
        —**Ming-Jer Chen, Leslie E. Grayson Professor of Business Administration, The Darden School, University of Virginia**

"An eloquent example of the fact that intercultural communication can have exceptional and enduring consequences."

—**George W. Renwick, president, Renwick and Associates**

"Impressive insights about cross-cultural communication. This book is highly recommended for those who do business in Japan and the global arena."

—**Kenichi Saito, professor, Kenichi Ohmae Graduate School of Business, former partner of McKinsey & Company, president, ForeSight & Company**

WITH RESPECT TO THE

JAPANESE

GOING TO WORK IN JAPAN

Second Edition

JOHN C. CONDON AND TOMOKO MASUMOTO

INTERCULTURAL PRESS
an imprint of Nicholas Brealey Publishing

BOSTON • LONDON

This edition first published by Intercultural Press, an imprint of Nicholas Brealey Publishing, in 2011.

20 Park Plaza, Suite 610
Boston, MA 02116, USA
Tel: + 617-523-3801
Fax: + 617-523-3708
www.interculturalpress.com

3-5 Spafield Street, Clerkenwell
London, EC1R 4QB, UK
Tel: +44-(0)-207-239-0360
Fax: +44-(0)-207-239-0370
www.nicholasbrealey.com

Printed in the United States of America

15   14   13   3   4   5

ISBN: 978-0-9842471-2-7

Library of Congress Cataloging-in-Publication Data

Condon, John C.
    With respect to the Japanese : going to work in Japan / John Condon and Tomoko Masumoto. — 2nd ed.
        p. cm.
    ISBN 978-0-9842471-2-7
1. National characteristics, Japanese.   2. Japan—Civilization.
3. Intercultural communication—Japan.   4. Business communication—
Japan.   I. Masumoto, Tomoko.   II. Title.
    DS821.C633 2010
    303.48'252073—dc22

                                                        2010038240

For Zac

CONTENTS

FOREWORD

When an earlier edition of this book was published in 1984, it quickly became a bible for Westerners seeking to understand and deal effectively with Japan, then considered the most competitive economy in the world. Now, nearly thirty years later, John C. Condon—with the collaboration of Tomoko Masumoto—has revised, updated, and expanded the classic book, this time aimed especially at Westerners who work in Japanese organizations.

Much in the world has changed since 1984. The fall of the Berlin Wall in 1989, the collapse of the Soviet Union in 1991, and the rise of the BRIC (Brazil, Russia, India, and China) economies have all contributed to the rapid globalization we are all witnessing. In the United States, few in the 1980s would have predicted the Internet boom and bust of the 1990s, the devastation of September 11, 2001, or the election of the nation's first African American president in 2008. Japan— usually considered a conservative and slowly changing society—saw the bursting of its real estate bubble in the early 1990s, the ensuing "lost decade" of economic stagnation, and, in 2009, a "regime change"—the election into office of the first genuine non-Liberal Democratic Party government in fifty-four years, seen by many as the most significant political event in postwar Japanese history.

Despite these momentous changes, continuities remain. The U.S. retains its position as the world's superpower, Japan remains a center of high technology and the world's second-largest economy measured in GDP, and the two countries are still close allies and partners. And, as was the case in the 1980s, the deeply rooted cultural differences between Japan and the U.S. (and the West) continue to impede communication, understanding, and cooperation, whether on the level of individuals, corporations, nonprofits, or governments.

That is why this book is so important. It provides an excellent guide for those who wish to understand differences between Japan and the West, and how to deal with them so that communication, collaboration, and cooperation can be improved. While reading this book, I found myself repeatedly nodding in agreement with the points being made, based on my lifetime of observing and participating in Japan's interactions with the West. Let me cite a few examples:

1. ***Honne* and *tatemae*.** The discussion in Chapter 3 of *honne* and *tatemae* and in Chapter 4 of 16 different ways to say "no" reminded me that this is one of the most fundamental sources of miscommunication and misunderstanding between Westerners and Japanese. The Anglo-American tradition of individualism, empiricism, and debate naturally leads many Westerners to want to focus on "the facts, nothing but the facts." The Japanese tradition of preserving group harmony and eschewing public confrontation and debate often leads to avoid saying "no" or to agree in principle but not necessarily on the specifics. This is a constant source of misunderstanding and even mistrust, when the Westerner later realizes that what he or she thought was a "yes" turned out to be merely a face-saving way to say "no." In a best-selling book published in 1989, a well-known Dutch journalist even went so far as to define *tatemae* as "socially sanctioned deceit."

2. **Oral expression.** The discussion in Chapter 4 of "Speech is silver, but silence is golden" reminded me of the following story. A Japanese friend of mine who spent one year as an AFS (American Field Service) exchange student in the U.S. told me that when she did not speak up in meetings at her American high school, her teachers and classmates considered her to be stupid (the American assumption was that her silence indicated ignorance). Upon returning to her high school in Tokyo, when she spoke up in meetings, her teachers and classmates considered her to be stupid (for not having enough Japanese common sense to maintain group harmony by staying silent). It is indeed difficult to appear intelligent in both societies while acting similarly in both, since there are values and actions considered desirable in one society—such as speaking up in the U.S.—that are considered undesirable in the other.

3. **Modesty.** The discussion in Chapter 4 of modesty reminded me of the following. In Japan, if a person appears to be overly confident of his or herself, he or she risks losing the support of others, since the attitude of many Japanese is, "If you're so confident of yourself, you certainly don't need my support." On the other hand, one of the surest ways to lose the support of Westerners is to appear to lack confidence, since the Western attitude is often, "How can we have confidence in you if you don't have confidence in yourself?" This explains, in part, the lack of confidence shown by some senior Japanese leaders when giving speeches, versus the supreme self-confidence displayed by even junior Westerners when making presentations. This tendency to

avoid exuding confidence can be a disadvantage to Japanese who are capable but modest when Westerners interview them for a promotion or for a new job.

4. **Time.** The discussion in Chapter 6 of time reminded me that Japanese are distinctively (some might say obsessively) punctual. In the West, it is considered normal to show up at dinners and parties "fashionably late"—a few minutes or (especially in southern Europe and Latin America) even an hour or more past the appointed time. In fact, showing up earlier could be embarrassing to the host, who may not have arrived at the restaurant or may be doing last-minute preparations at home. However, in Japan, guests usually show up exactly at the appointed time, or even earlier, to show their respect for the host. Thus, Japanese are often irritated at Westerners for being so rude as to show up late, whereas Westerners are often annoyed at Japanese for being so inconsiderate as to show up early. Each is trying to be polite and considerate to the other, but not being understood or appreciated.

5. **Human relationships.** The discussion in Chapter 6 of time and relationships correctly highlights the fact that Japanese tend to value long-term human relationships more than do many Westerners. And these relationships can importantly affect one's success doing business in Japan. Whereas many Westerners view business as a series of spot transactions unrelated to each other based purely on objective economic criteria such as price, many Japanese base business decisions in part on the trust and confidence they have in their counterparts, since service, maintenance, and reliability include human factors in addition to the quality of the product being sold. In addition, in Japan, Company A may make certain concessions to Company B on the expectation that, in the future, Company B will reciprocate. But such implicit deals can work only if there is shared memory between the companies, based on the continuity of relationships between individuals over time.

These are just a few of the many examples from my experiences that came to mind as I was reading this valuable book. My examples may seem trivial, but as explained by Condon and Masumoto, small differences on the surface can hide more fundamental differences based on upbringing, education, culture, and values. And these differences can lead to profound business, economic, political, and national security consequences.

Of course, globalization is having its impact on Japan. With more foreigners and foreign direct investment in Japan and with more Japanese spending time abroad, it is increasingly difficult to draw hard-and-fast lines between "Japanese" and "non-Japanese." Indeed, some younger Japanese who have spent long periods of time abroad are individualistic rather than group-oriented, self-assertive rather than modest, articulate in foreign languages rather than reticent, and combative rather than harmonious. But these individuals are still the exception in Japan, especially outside of Tokyo.

So, for Westerners who deal with the mainstream of Japan, this book is highly recommended. It will sensitize readers to differences between Japan and the West, explain why these differences exist, and suggest how to overcome them. It is an invaluable guide to promote communication, understanding, and cooperation between Westerners and Japanese.

Glen S. Fukushima
Former President, American Chamber of Commerce in Japan

Glen S. Fukushima is President and CEO of Airbus Japan. An American of Japanese ancestry who grew up in a bilingual and bicultural environment, he was educated at Stanford, Harvard, Keio, and Tokyo University. His career has spanned academia, journalism, law, government, and business. He has worked for one European and four American global companies and served as Vice President and President of the American Chamber of Commerce in Japan from 1993 to 1999.

PREFACE

The first edition of this book was written primarily for people from the United States who were looking for some information and guidance about working with people from Japan. The reader would have been aware that challenges invariably arise when people from different backgrounds, with sometimes very different life experiences and social values, attempt to communicate with mutual respect.

We hope this new edition will be of interest and helpful to the same imagined reader as well as many Westerners. The revised and expanded form of this book is directed especially to readers who are seriously considering, or are actively involved in, going to work in Japan, in Japanese organizations, and conversing to some extent in the Japanese language. Such potential readers would have been rare at the time of the earlier edition of this book, but today they number in the thousands.

As Glen Fukushima describes in his splendid Foreword to this edition, both Japan and the United States—and their manifold relationships—have changed considerably since the first edition was published. Along with dramatic political and economic changes is a history of increased social contact between people from Japan and the U.S., Canada, Europe, and elsewhere. Crossing the ocean today to study, for a short visit, or for work is not at all unusual, and even when staying at home, daily contacts via the internet to people, information, and myriad images have made what felt distant decades ago now feel closer, even familiar. The Japanese government's efforts to promote *kokusaika* (internationalization) have also been effective, both in Japan and abroad. Tens of thousands of non-Japanese have made an impact in school classrooms and local government offices throughout Japan through the auspices of the Japan Exchange and Teaching (JET) Program. In the realm of business, engineering, and science, thousands of people have been part of a number of internship programs, which provide opportunities for many serious people from abroad to enter Japanese organizations for periods of a few months to a few years. Their ages ranged from early twenties to late fifties and included many with considerable work experience as engineers, scientists, and in business organizations; several had advanced degrees.

Tomoko Masumoto has studied the experiences of these expatriate workers, mostly in the role of "intern," and those of their Japanese coworkers and supervisors for more than a decade, and findings and insights from her work pervade this new edition. Indeed, one of the most striking findings is the similarity of initial challenges experienced irrespective of age and experience. As with so much of intercultural communication, problems may arise less from our ignorance of where we are going to work than from ignorance of our own values, assumptions, and expectations acquired in the experience of where we are coming from. The men and women from the United States and Canada who were interviewed in this research ranged in age from their twenties to their mid-forties. Most had work experience, some with many years in positions of responsibility. Many were engineers and scientists who worked in laboratories; others came to Japan to gain experience working in company offices. Nearly all had some preparation about Japanese culture and had studied, to varying degrees, the Japanese language. Though each person's experience was unique there was remarkable consistency among the challenges, frustrations, and satisfactions they described. Even those people who had studied Japanese culture and management in college reacted similarly to those who had much less preparation. The reason is because intercultural communication is at least as much about one's own personal and cultural background, values, assumptions, and expectations as it is about studying how things work in another culture.

It is helpful to keep in mind that each of us is like no other person—we are each unique in our experience, hopes, and behavior. Some find it a wonder that we communicate as well as we do, even with others in our own family. However, because of each person's individual qualities of temperament, personality, and even sense of humor, we can form bonds of friendship with people who otherwise would seem to have little in common with us if we only paid attention to our different cultural backgrounds.

It is also true that each of us is like all other people—at some fundamental level we share much, which is one reason why we can respond to works of art and literature created at very different times and places. This book is about intercultural communication, not interspecies or intergalactic communication. Intercultural communication assumes that each of us is more likely to share assumptions, expectations, and behavior with those with whom we share a similar upbringing and social history. It is here, however, that we must urge caution about some of the categories used in discussing intercultural relations. People may share a nationality and language but differ considerably across generations, particularly in societies that have undergone great changes within a lifetime. A new Japanese employee reared by parents who grew up during Japan's bubble economy does not have the same experience as a Japanese manager whose parents lived through the war and post-war period. The life experience of women is not the same as that of men, irrespective of nationality. There may be ethnic, racial, and religious differences within a society, including Japan; there are regional differences, urban and rural differences, and many more that should give pause when speaking of "the Japanese" or "the Canadians" or about those from the U.S. or anywhere else. All the more so with a word like "Westerner." In Japan today there are many people from other Asian countries and from South America who work in factories and who provide other services including in the field of healthcare. We can all learn from studies of their experiences, too, but this book is written about and for those who have gone to Japan primarily from North America and Europe.

In the realm of everyday or popular culture, even people who are not particularly interested in Japan may be familiar with many Japanese foods, martial arts, and, today especially, manga and anime. Indeed, as we note in the book, a principal attraction for many of those who want to go to work in Japan is spurred by an initial attraction to anime, manga, and related graphic genres more than by the motivation to learn about Japanese organizational communication and management. But as Glen Fukushima also affirms, intercultural communication challenges persist with an impressive consistency. Our research indicates that even those who take Japanese language classes, study about many aspects of Japanese culture and society, and participate in workshops or training programs in intercultural communication are still likely to confront everyday challenges when they go to work in Japan. Almost certainly their presence in the organization will also pose challenges for their Japanese coworkers, supervisors, and friends.

In this new edition, we try to draw attention to these everyday issues, particularly those that are noted during the first months and years of going to work in Japan. We hope that in some small way this book can contribute to the goal of working across cultures with increased understanding, encouragement, and, always, with respect.

John C. Condon
Tomoko Masumoto

ACKNOWLEDGMENTS

Acknowledging the many people who contribute to all that goes into a book is important, risky, and bound to be incomplete. It is important for the obvious reasons, risky because names will be left out in an effort to limit numbers or through oversight soon regretted. Even a very long list will ultimately be incomplete; we are influenced by people whose names we never knew, and by those whose words or actions take on special significance only after time.

There are a number of organizations and people who we wish to thank for their assistance in making this book possible. Research support was provided by agencies of the governments of the United States and Japan, including the Japanese Ministry of Education, Culture, Sports, Science, and Technology, and the Grants-in-Aid for Scientific Research. Many individuals, including Alexander DeAngelis and Randall Soderquist of the National Science Foundation, Koto White of the U.S. Air Force Office of Scientific Research, and Hiro Kanda and Minoru Umemoto of the Japan External Trade Organization, kindly gave information and assistance in the study of the JIMT programs.

We would also like to thank many of the people who were deeply involved in university internship programs, including the directors and coordinators who generously offered information and personal reflections about their programs; they also provided valuable introductions to the students whom they helped go to work in Japan. These include a dear friend and wise colleague at the University of New Mexico, the late Everett Rogers. We also want to thank Daniela Reichert, Director of Intern Placement at the MIT Japan program; Eiko Fujioka Rutherford, former coordinator at the Stanford Japan Center; Jenny Kagetsu, Director of the Canada-Japan Co-op Program, and Yuko Nemoto, Assistant Coordinator, at the University of British Columbia; Wallace Lopez, Co-Director of the Asian Technology Information Program; Dean Collinwood, Director of the U.S.-Japan and China Centers at the University of Utah; and Michio Tsutsui, Director of the Technical Japanese Program at the University of Washington.

Acknowledgments

We wish to thank Erika Heilman and Jennifer Olsen at Intercultural Press and Nicholas Brealey Publishing for their kind encouragement and for their professional advice. And we want to say thank you to Kichiro Hayashi and to Glen and Sakie Fukushima for the wisdom they have shared over many years of friendship, with special thanks to Glen for his kindness in writing such a eloquent and helpful Foreword to this book.

Finally, we want to thank the dozens of current and former interns from the United States and Canada with whom we spent many rewarding hours as they shared stories of their experiences of working in Japan, times difficult and times precious. For sharing their memories, advice, and also their lingering uncertainties, we wish to express our deepest gratitude. Their names must remain anonymous, but we hope readers find the insights and encouragement they offer throughout this book helpful.

John C. Condon
Tomoko Masumoto

All I Really Need to Know,
They Learned in Kindergarten

In *All I Really Need to Know I Learned in Kindergarten*, a best-selling book in the United States some years ago, author Robert Fulghum wrote of the simple wisdom of learning to share everything, hold hands, and stick together when crossing the street. The book reminded millions that so much of what we value and share was given shape when we were just five or six years old. Decades before Fulghum's delightful book, a revealing study was conducted by researchers in Japan in which children's behavior in U.S. and international school kindergartens was compared with that of Japanese children in their kindergartens.

A team of Japanese and American researchers visited several kindergartens in Japan. These included American schools and international schools strongly influenced by U.S. schools (in staffing, curriculum, language used, and enrollment). Others were *yōchien*, Japanese kindergartens. The researchers were interested in children's drawings. They wondered if, given the same instructions, the children from different cultures would make significantly different pictures. If Michael drew a picture of the sun, for example, would he color it yellow while Mariko's sun would be colored red, just like the sun in her country's flag? The answer, as it turned out, was a resounding "yes," so much so that almost anybody could sort through the hundreds of drawings and nearly always guess which

1

were done by Japanese children and which were drawn by North American, Australian, and some European children.

But as culture is more a process than its products, more an event than an object, the truly revealing differences appeared in how the children made their pictures. If we take a closer look at what happened when these children were asked to "draw a picture of your family," we can learn a good deal about Japanese and other ways of looking at the world and doing things. We can also anticipate some of the problems that can result when people from different cultures attempt to work together.

To begin with, the seating arrangements in each school were different. In some American classrooms there were individual desks, while in others the children sat on the floor. In all of the Japanese kindergartens, however, the children sat around tables in groups of six or eight.

The roles of the teachers were also different. When the researchers visited a school to ask the children to draw the pictures, the American teachers invited the visitors to "go right ahead and tell the boys and girls what you want them to do." In the Japanese schools, however, all communication was handled by the teacher who remained the authority, the responsible person, and the go-between. "Tell me what you want me to tell the children," the teacher would say.

How the children began and how they carried out the activity also differed. Usually, as soon as an American child received a sheet of paper he or she would begin to draw. When the picture was finished, the child would hold it up to be collected or would bring it to the teacher's desk. In the Japanese schools the children waited until all of the papers had been distributed. Then, at each table, the children looked at each other and talked a little about what they were supposed to do. Then, table by table, and almost as if by signal, all the children would begin to draw. Throughout the activity, children would turn and look at what the others were doing. Those who finished first waited until the others were done, and when all were finished the drawings were collected.

When children showed difficulty in drawing someone in the family, the responses of the teachers were also different. The Japanese teacher would usually assist the child, not infrequently taking the child's hand and guiding the crayon. (This is truly "hands-on learning!" It is the same method used to teach Japanese children other skills, such as writing and bowing.) In the American schools, the teachers encouraged the children with words: "Just do your best" or "It's your father and your picture, and you should try to draw him the way you see him."

Finally, the order in which the family members were drawn was also notably different. For the Japanese youngsters, the order usually began with father, then mother, then older brother or sister. The child would draw himself or herself next, and if there were still younger siblings, they would be drawn last. For the American children and those from other countries, the order seemed much more random. The only notable tendency was for some of the children from the U.S. to draw themselves first.

In short, there were cultural differences in the physical arrangements of the classrooms, the kind of contact with an outsider that was allowed, the extent of coordination in the beginning and ending of tasks, the role of the person in charge of the activity and the kind of instruction that person offered, and the depiction of social relationships, the "social order." Each of these themes is worth a closer look, for together with other themes, they characterize some of the major features that contrast the different cultures and are at the heart of many of the confusions, challenges, and conflicts that arise when people from overseas come to work in Japan.

Had the researchers been able to observe children in elementary school, they would have seen some of this behavior expressed in other ways as well. Each week, different groups of Japanese students would have the responsibility to arrive at the classroom early, perhaps write each day's date on the board, greet their teacher when she or he arrives, and try to be helpful. At the end of the day others remain and clean the board and tidy up the room. There might well be one group with the responsibility to help serve lunch to their classmates, a practice common in public schools throughout Japan in many grades, as hot lunches are prepared and provided for all students. The value of one's responsibility to others in the group and to the maintenance of the group begins outside of the family when Japanese children first go to school, and is apparent again two decades later when they first enter a company, research laboratory, or other organization.

Institutions and organizations are cultural products, shaped by cultural values that are explicit and espoused as well as others that are more subtle, and shaped through one's own experience that has been shared with others and thus more likely to be reproduced. Intentionally, but also less consciously, much of "what we really need to know" to fit in and feel comfortable in an organization includes a lot of what we learned when we were four or five years old, or even younger.

"I" OR "WE"

Every person, everywhere, is both an individual, physically separate from others, but also connected to others emotionally and in many ways dependent on others throughout life. Cultural background influences which of these characteristics—

the independent individual or the interdependent group member—is given emphasis when we think of ourselves. In countless ways, both obvious and subtle, the Japanese are encouraged to think first of their relationship with others: "We" before "I." We of this family, we of this school, we of this nation, or just "we" who are together in a room talking. One is never fully independent; one must always be conscious of others.

For many from other cultural backgrounds, the individual, not the group, is basic. So many of the beliefs and values—equality, democracy, freedom, privacy, and even progress—that are espoused (if not always deeply felt), are bound up with a particular view of individualism. Cooperation and teamwork are important, to be sure, but these should arise from the choice and desire of the individual. From this perspective, groups are important, but they are composed of individuals who should be wary of groups that exert too much personal or social influence on the individuals.

These are not simply interesting cultural differences. They are very emotional issues. A visitor may become upset if a Japanese expresses an opinion beginning with "*Wareware nihonjin*" ("We Japanese"). "Just give me your own opinion," an American may insist. Likewise, Japanese find some expressions of American individualism rude and antisocial. Americans tend to speak in terms of "in my opinion," "I think," and so on, in order to be both personal and also cautious about speaking for others. Nevertheless, the impression given can be one of egotism. Ironically, each may intend to be showing a kind of modesty: Saying "we" can be a way of subordinating one's own view, and saying "in my view" may be a way of indicating one doesn't presume to speak for others.

If one identifies strongly with a group, it is especially important to maintain good relations and avoid conflicts with others in the group. Even away from the group—the family, school, or business—one must be careful not to act in such a way that might cause embarrassment to the group.

In Japan, school loyalties last a long time, and when one joins an organization, like a company, the hope, if not expectation, is that this identification will also last a long time. Transferring from school to school or company to company was rare before the bursting of the bubble economy in the 1990s, and it is still not common. To be required to change because of forces outside of one's control is one thing; to want to change is something else. It may suggest that the person might not have been able to get along well with others and raises questions about how well the person can fit into the new situation. Changing is also discouraged because the person who enters laterally simply will not be able to draw from experiences shared with others who have been together for a longer time. Changing one's affiliation from one school to another or from one company to another is perceived as disruptive; it doesn't contribute to the harmony of the group.

Efforts to maintain harmony are reflected in many ways, including cautious and indirect speech, taking time to sense another's mood before venturing an opinion, and avoiding as much as possible public disagreement. The experience in the Japanese kindergarten also showed two other important means of ensuring harmony: the use of a go-between and the coordination of actions. We explore these themes elsewhere in the book.

HIRING PRACTICES

Japanese employees are hired as a group or "class," once a year, much like students entering a school. Though their activities may differ, they work together, eat together, and some may live together in a company dormitory. The ability to get along with others is therefore a very important criterion for being hired. Character, along with family background and school attended, usually count for much more than specialized training or outstanding personal abilities, for these could work against one's ability to fit in comfortably. For example, a Japanese-American was being interviewed for a position with a major Japanese corporation known throughout the world. The student had lived in Japan for many years and was fluent in both English and Japanese. Each of the persons who interviewed the candidate was apparently most concerned about his American background, for each stressed "there is no room for individualism in this company."

Another young Japanese employee of a prestigious trading company became disillusioned with company policies after about one year. He was an idealist and some of what went on did not conform to his principles. He considered what few Japanese fortunate enough to work for the company would have contemplated: leaving the company and perhaps returning to graduate school and then going into teaching. He sought advice from many people and finally decided to remain. What most persuaded him to stay? "I realized," he told this writer, with whom he had studied in college, "that if I left the company, it would make it much more difficult for others from this college to be hired by the company in the future."

Not all Japanese follow the pattern of graduating from school and going directly into the workforce of companies and organizations where they may work for the next four decades. At the height of "the bubble" people began to realize that there were many—a small percent but noticeable—young people in Japan who were unable to find a suitable job. Others chose not to follow the

5

path toward lifetime employment but rather to follow a more independent path by taking modest service, low-wage jobs, such as in the popular convenience stores (*konbini*) that are in every neighborhood, in fast-food outlets, or in other places that employ large numbers of people who work part time (*arubaito*), often while completing college. Called *freeters*, (*frītā*), they comprise a small percent of workers, but they are an important part of the workforce.

DECISION MAKING

In most cases, Japanese prefer making decisions by consensus rather than by voting. People should talk and talk until some agreement emerges. If the mood is such that no consensus seems possible, then it may be best to defer making a decision. Though Americans may not be unhappy to reach consensus, voting is a part of the American way—even in schoolrooms and in homes. One person, one vote: this preserves the rights of the individual. From this perspective it may risk little, when it becomes apparent there are different opinions on matters requiring a decision, to say, "Let's vote on it." But where the group values are especially strong, asking one to "stand up and be counted" can feel very threatening to everyone and to the intricate and often delicate strands that maintain the integrity of the group. Better to defer a decision and continue to talk—often about another topic—with the hope that a consensus can be reached and a vote avoided or, when taken, serve as the formal affirmation of a decision reached through hours of informal discussion.

Of course, not all that anyone needs to know was learned in kindergarten, but some of the key cultural features are expressed there and reinforced in schools, the institution that is one of the first encountered outside of the family. Some of these key features run through this book as we consider interpersonal relations in Japanese companies, schools, and other organizations: (1) the centrality of the group; (2) sensitivity to relative age, seniority, and rank (Chapter 2); (3) the significance of the *sekininsha* or responsible person (Chapters 2 and 3), and the setting and physical arrangement that helps define the group and exerts an influence on everyday communication in the workplace (Chapter 5); and the coordination of activities, beginnings and endings, and attention to form (Chapter 4). This book describes how these groups are formed and how these relationships characterize the strong bonds in organizations that are omnipresent in Japanese society, and focuses on the challenges that someone from overseas is likely to encounter when going to work in Japan. These can be formidable, especially if one is unaware of how he or she "fits" into the organization. How we experience and use space and time (Chapter 6) are crucial features of every culture, and yet most people are not aware of their significance until encountering the unfamiliar. Learning through the feedback given by others (Chapter 7), and learning at work when the anticipated feedback appears lacking (Chapter 8). We will expand on some of the behavior that is literally "commonly sensed" in Japan, what most Japanese—even of different generations—would have experienced, and the resulting values and expectations that others will share. This extends even to annual events that hold personal and cultural meanings and give shape to the year (Chapter 9).

TWO

The Social Order

From the perspective of many who come from abroad to work in Japan, Japanese people are excessively conscious of one's status relative to one another, and especially to age and seniority. This sensitivity is not unknown elsewhere, of course. Attention to age differences is greater elsewhere—in Korean culture, for example. Across cultures, often the challenge is not so much something completely new but rather something that looks familiar but seems like it is either not appreciated enough or is overdone. For many from the U.S., Australia, and other more individualistic-valuing societies, the Japanese respect for the social order can be an issue. Complaints or sarcasm by newcomers about "the chain of command" in Japan was among the most frequent comments about their experience of working in Japan. For many Westerners, this aspect of the social order in Japan may look like a bit too much attention to hierarchy (and it sometimes can be) but in Japan it is experienced, felt, and valued as order and security.

There are many ways in which the Japanese publicly acknowledge a social hierarchy: in the use of language, in seating arrangements at social gatherings, in bowing to one another, and in hundreds of other ways. Watch Japanese greet each other and the principles are apparent in the sometimes subtle differences in near-synchronous behavior. Notice who bows lower, who waits for the other to go first, and who apologizes more. The deferential order is: (1) younger defers to older; (2) in a school club, company, or other organization, deference is shown to seniority; and (3) those seeking a favor will bow lower than those whose favor is sought; for example, the seller bows to the customer. Gender may come into play, though less so than in the past, and in ways sometimes puzzling to the outsider, as we will note later in this chapter.

All of this can be a source of discomfort for those with more egalitarian values. For one thing, the very words used in attempting to describe the patterns may be emotionally loaded: "superior" and "subordinate." It is not uncommon for outsiders to infer that if differences are stressed, then one must always be viewed as better than the other. Understanding is further complicated because, as some Japanese scholars have argued in recent years, the discussion of the "horizontal" in Japanese human relations has often been minimized or overlooked, just as the "vertical" in more apparently egalitarian societies tends to be ignored (issues of social class, for example), in part because it complicates a simple description of a cultural value system.

Each system must be viewed on its own terms and not on the expectations of the other. In the case of deference due to age, for example, not only the social system but the language, aesthetic sensitivity, and historic influences reflect the same respect for one who is older. The Japanese language has no single word for *brother*, for example; there are words for older brother and younger brother, and for older sister and younger sister, but not for just *sister*. Moreover, in the family the older brothers and sisters will be called by those terms, rather than by their given names. Being older does not, however, mean that one can do what one pleases. Older brother or older sister has special responsibilities toward parents and toward the younger ones. Being older is not necessarily an enviable position. The younger is able to depend upon and lean on the older for support, a pattern that holds true among schoolmates of different ages as well. This is the *senpai-kōhai* (senior-junior) bond, which continues long after college and extends into the business world, with favors sought and granted between the former students who are bound together because of—not in spite of—their differences in age.

In an organization, being sensitive to one's age or seniority relative to someone else gives a person a sense of security and guides how one communicates with others, which is essential for harmonious human relations. A younger person may be more able than an older person, and it may be that others recognize that without having to be shown, but the younger will still show deference to the older.

In the case of a Japanese student and teacher, the student bows to his or her teacher at school and on the street out of respect for the role of teachers and respect for education in the society. Years later, if that former student should become, say, prime minister, and if he or she should again meet the teacher on the street, the former student will still bow low to the former teacher. It is not a matter of who is more famous or powerful but a matter of acknowledging one's proper place in a system, which helps to maintain reasonably harmonious human relations in a crowded land.

In intercultural encounters, however, things can get mixed up. A fifty-nine-year-old Japanese vice president of a Japanese bank may meet to discuss something with a Canadian vice president of the Tokyo branch of a Canadian bank and find that the Canadian is only thirty-nine years old. When they meet, should their bowing reflect their different ages or their identical rank? Will the Japanese vice president have any misgivings about a Canadian organization that sends such a young representative? Does the difference in age reflect the Canadian hierarchy of branches and affiliates? This is the stuff of diplomacy. It should be noted that some of the awkwardness in such a situation is reduced if the two converse in English, which requires less fine tuning to fit each social situation than does Japanese.

SENPAI AND KŌHAI

Three words describe the vital relationships: *senpai, kōhai,* and *dōki. Senpai* refers to a person who is one's senior and *kōhai* to one's junior in the organization. There is also the very important relationship with someone in one's cohort who entered at the same time (*dōki*). Japan has been famously called a "vertical society" (*tate shakai*) by Tokyo University anthropologist Chie Nakane, and indeed the importance of attention to many markers of hierarchy is a significant feature of the culture. Deference to age and to seniority and attention to the hierarchical structure of an organization in everyday communication, all contribute to the solidarity and maintenance of the group. There is also the "horizontal dimension," which is equally important though it tends to receive less recognition.

This seniority system is not unique to Japanese organizations, of course, but the bonds that develop between senpai and kōhai are remarkably strong and enduring. Normally one's senpai is someone who is older than and/or has more experience than the kōhai, who is younger or has less experience. Throughout school, junior high school and high school especially, if one is part of a club or sports team, one refers to the teammate who is older as his or her senpai, and to one's teammate who entered later and is younger as his or her kōhai. During school years, especially if one belongs to a school sports club during junior high school and high school, this senpai-kōhai relationship is distinct and is apparent in words of address and in behavior. Members' duties and opportunities within the club largely depend on their relative status in the club, so that even if a freshman in a sports club has abilities superior to all the seniors, he or she will still be assigned menial duties—and would feel very uncomfortable if it were otherwise. A similar pattern occurs in the workplace, with the new hires usually performing seemingly menial though essential tasks, typically for the entire first year. In their first year in the company they may unpack boxes, distribute mail within the organization, and so on. They may also be expected to arrive at the office earlier than others in order to organize documents or even to clean up the office. (At year end, though, even senior workers participate in cleaning.) Of course, not all of the cleaning is done this way; most companies also employ janitors.

When speaking of an acquaintance in another division or even another company who might be helpful when seeking some information, an employee might say, "Oh, I have a senpai over there," or "My kōhai works there," rather than just saying, "I have a friend there" or "I know someone who works there." The vertical bond is a strong and valuable one.

In most organizations there is a fit between relative age and seniority, as most employees enter an organization right out of college, and most entered college at the same age or within about a year of the same age. Thus one's senpai would almost always be older and one's kōhai younger. But disruptions in the normal order of things, such as the two-decade economic downturn that led to people being laid off and considerable "restructuring," meant that many Japanese who found work at a new company entered at, say, age thirty-two rather than the usual age of twenty-three or twenty-four, which meant that their new senpai were often younger than they were. This creates some awkwardness in adjustment for all concerned.

The senpai-kōhai relationship can have a strong emotional quality as well. In Chie Nakane's classic explanation, in order to be a member of a group, such as a high school sports club, a newcomer needs to have a person who introduces the new person to the group. The other members in the group accept the newcomer because of the recommendation, and the new member feels deeply indebted to the person who made it all possible. Thus, as part of the emotional bond, as University of Hawaii anthropologist Takie Sugiyama Lebra and others have pointed out, a feeling of dependency may play an important role. The sempai-kōhai relationship, analogous to the parent-child relationship, is also apparent in

Japanese organizations. The kōhai can expect to depend upon his or her senpai for security and help, and sometimes even for protection, much as one might appeal to a parent for emotional support at a time of need.

DŌKI

Every April, Japanese organizations welcome new employees who have just graduated from college. A large company may hire hundreds of new employees every year. Dōki literally means "same term" and *dōkisei* (or dōki) refers to people who joined a company or school in the same year. Because of the Japanese educational system, most of the new employees will be of approximately the same age. These new hires spend anywhere from a few days up to a few months training together. After each is assigned to a division, the dōki continue to have gatherings and training programs throughout their entire first year. Some may have a third year of training for a few days, and there are other kinds of training, such as leadership training for fifth-year employees. Especially through the training that takes place the first year, these dōki strengthen the connection with all the people who joined the company at the same time they did.

Because people from abroad who study about Japan and who may want to go to work in Japan learn so much about the vertical dimension in Japanese relationships, the significance of dōki has often been overlooked. Many of the interns in our research indicate that they had heard so much about the importance of junior-senior relations that some were surprised when they discovered the significance of the dōki. Their supervisors were surprised that the interns hadn't appreciated the strength of the dōki relationships.

One research scientist from the United States who worked in a team with about thirty others said this about his coworkers:

> People seem to get along and are cheerful almost all of the time here in Japan. I know that each morning people are going to be in a good mood and are going to be constant. Here [in Japan] people are friendliest with their dōki and their teammates—people they see frequently. In America, there is no system like that, so people make friends with whomever they feel like.

Because dōki are assigned to different divisions and then are moved from one division to another during their early years in the company, one's dōki network soon becomes widespread in the organization. Though not appearing in any formal organizational chart, the networks of dōki are a major force in the cohesiveness and solidarity of Japanese organizations.

WANTING TO FIT IN

The senpai-kōhai and dōki relationships form a social grid of human relations in the company, school, or other organizations where people have worked together and expect to continue to do so for some time. But what are the possibilities for someone who has come to Japan for a relatively short period and who, in many ways, is not and may never be a part of the organization as his or her Japanese colleagues are? Often the Japanese model holds, but sometimes in innovative or improvised ways because the situation of a non-Japanese in a short-term, unconventional role is often novel for all concerned.

Here is the experience of many North American interns who joined Japanese companies for a period of from six months to two years. Many of these interns were seasoned professionals with years of experience working in private and government laboratories or for large corporations. When they arrived at their organization, the interns were assigned instructors or other employees, including peer workers, who served as their senpai. These employees played the role of mentor and offered the interns access to the network channels that are so important. Through the assistance and encouragement of their instructors or their "functional senpai," the interns were able to develop interpersonal relationships while learning about the inner workings of the organization during and after work hours.

It helps considerably if one can enter a Japanese organization at the same time that the new and committed Japanese employees enter, because when Japanese employees join a company, they are all together during their training, and it is during this time that they begin to build networks across divisions, exchanging information even during lunch and after the regular work hours.

It is one's senpai who acts as a bridge to link an outsider to insiders and fosters stronger ties with people who share similar interests or responsibilities. In this regard, newcomers who can connect with someone who is closer in age and who can speak English, and with new Japanese employees whose positions are similar to theirs, find it much easier to become integrated into the organization than those who work mainly with older, formally assigned instructors. This is what most of the people who have gone to work in Japan report, and it fits with decades of studies' findings of what—or who—makes the biggest difference when the newcomer enters the group.

Because of the likely struggle with the Japanese language, newcomers usually need someone who can help. Most Japanese colleagues cannot do much to help, but having someone to turn to and ask questions in English greatly reduces one's anxiety as a non-Japanese working in a Japanese organization. These people voluntarily helped the interns. Usually it is necessary for the person who has not grown up in Japan to take the initiative to ask for help and to develop relationships with people who can help. Officially assigned supervisors may be helpful in this role, but they may lack the linguistic and intercultural capability to do so. In our study, few interns regarded their supervisors as mentors. Interns reported that, in general, the supervisors did not work that closely with them, though they did observe the interns in their work and showed concern about personal matters, such as their health. (Interviews with the Japanese supervisors revealed backstage roles that were sometimes crucial but in ways the newcomers were never aware of.) People who are assigned to be instructors often are so busy with their own work and other responsibilities that they cannot be expected to do all that a newcomer might want or need.

HOW IT WORKS: REQUESTING PERMISSION

Now comes the hard part. It is not so difficult to get a general idea of the vertical and horizontal relationships in the organization, and even to appreciate how important these are. It can be another matter for someone working within the organization, especially when he or she wants to request something of personal importance. A dispassionate appreciation of the vertical structure can give way to a passionate description of what it feels like for Westerners to work in a system that does not seem to be irritating for the Japanese coworkers. The expatriates talked about dealing with "the chain of command:"

> Japanese communication seems very dependent on respect for the hierarchy of seniority, building of mutual consensus, and group harmony. Concerning hierarchy of seniority, I am talking about the very structured arrangement of Japanese management systems. I have never seen or heard of a younger person as a superior, or higher level of authority, with someone who is older than them. As a consequence, the younger employee is always talking to the older employee from a low position. In America I do not really care about the person's age or gender; all I need to know is who is my boss; whom do I need to take my orders from? In that respect, I do not think age is as great a consideration in American management systems as it is in Japan. Here in the Japanese system I cannot freely contact anyone

I may choose. I have to go through the proper "channels" or "go through the chain of command," as one might say in the military.

For example, if I would like to leave early, I must first ask my group senpai who will then ask my *kachō* [division chief] who would then tell my senpai who will tell me. From an American point of view, instead of wasting my senpai's time, I should just ask my kachō directly. Asking when I could leave my internship and return to the U.S., I had to ask my senpai, who arranged a meeting with my *buchō* [department director], who then asked the person responsible for me in Human Resources. Again, as an American I view this as a waste of time. However, in both these cases I think this way of communication . . . [shows the importance of] giving the proper respect to those who are my superiors.

A woman from the United States described an early experience at her Tokyo company: "I was told to clean up one of the workrooms that my team uses. But this order first came from my *shochō* [director], who told my team leader, who told my everyday boss, who then told me. Here one never goes directly to anyone."

An observant and thoughtful person from the U.S. whom we asked about his experience said this:

Western expatriates working even longer periods in Japan expressed frustration that seemingly simple matters had to be presented formally and then passed around to many people. For the Americans this appeared "inefficient," and an example of what they interpreted as excessively hierarchical, "bureaucratic." What they considered to be more "practical" and "efficient" ways of doing things were, they learned, not how things work in Japanese organizations. Their awareness became clearest when they observed how their own requests were handled and, in some cases, how they misjudged the importance of the hierarchical flow.

Whatever one believes to be more "efficient" or "more practical" ways of doing things is not necessarily how things work in organizations where management styles and business practices are shaped by a primary group orientation and attention to the hierarchies that maintain the group. This appreciation for how the network of relationships functions should also help those who may never work in Japan but work with Japanese organizations. Things take time because more people are involved in being informed—even if they are not actually responsible for a decision—than an outsider might imagine.

THE RESPONSIBLE PERSON

When the teacher acted as a buffer between the children in the kindergarten class and the visitors as described in Chapter 1, she did so for at least two reasons: for one, she served as a go-between to deflect direct contact between people that might otherwise be awkward, confusing, or disruptive. More importantly, in this situation she was the *sekininsha*, the responsible person. Awareness of who has the responsibility for someone or something, especially if problems arise, is never far from mind in a Japanese organization. Sometimes the responsibility falls mainly to the person in charge (*tantōsha*), but the responsibility also extends upward in the organizational network.

Good intentions, such as not wanting to bother a senior person who is very busy with some matter that seems minor, can have bad effects. Matters that may seem personal and none of the organization's business, such as wanting to buy a car, may be viewed differently by those who have responsibilities for the expat worker. The "personal" request may require a sequence of notifications and approvals before the request is finally granted—or not. Even at universities, senior professors who have been at the school for decades usually must inform the administration when they leave for vacation and say where they are going.

ROLES

"It's like the difference between basketball and baseball," management professor and author Kichiro Hayashi has said in explaining the differences in how Japanese think of their roles in an organization. While baseball players are hired for specific roles—the pitcher pitches, the catcher catches, each outfielder has his domain—in basketball one is also hired for abilities and has an area to maintain, the game is fluid, and everyone must be able to act when needed. Teamwork comes before role. One does not often hear "that's not my responsibility" in Japan.

Japanese will tell you that one of the most challenging things about travel in Western countries is tipping taxi drivers, workers at restaurants, and those who assist at hotels and airports. The idea of rewarding someone for doing what should be just normal behavior or their work makes no sense. And doubly bothersome: why? And then, what? Something like these feelings also may characterize the cultural division between "my job" (expressed more often as "not my job") and "our" work, plan, or project. Japanese supervisors are shocked when interns or other new employees assume such role boundaries. The cultural values of "I" and "we" can emerge in many contexts.

REGARDING GENDER

At every level of individual identity and interpersonal relationships gender is an important consideration. Certainly one cannot look at roles and relationships in an organization without giving attention to gender. That said, it is also true that to try to describe the roles of men and women without also considering other factors risks forming or reinforcing generalizations that form stereotypical images that, like all stereotypes, are belied by actual experience. This is especially true for the newcomer who can recognize gender but has little knowledge of a person's age, educational background, history of working within the organization, social status, marital and parental status, as well as other less apparent factors that may be far more relevant than gender alone. National and international influences that affect many aspects of culture, including gender, must be taken into account: this includes the national and even international economic landscape and the technological innovations and social and political forces that can alter roles and relationships seemingly overnight. Each company or other organization has its own history, policies, and practices which affect roles and relationships in the organization. Beyond, or perhaps before, all of these are the personal experiences, values, and aspirations of each person one meets and works with in the office, lab, or other workplace. Each person has his or her own story and aspirations which may or may not conform to what someone else might assume and expect. Our interviews suggest that many newcomers arrive with certain fixed notions about gender in Japan today, images which are often over-generalized or outdated in a Japan that continues to change.

For these reasons, the person who comes from abroad to go to work in Japan is advised to take care in making assumptions about coworkers and relationships with coworkers solely on the basis of gender. One engineer who came from the U.S. to work in Japan had expected that most women at the lab would be assistants or do mostly clerical work. To his surprise, his section leader and supervisor was female, with a Ph.D. and years of professional experience. Still, he also saw many women whom he knew had an educational background comparable to his doing work that seemed rather rudimentary, and he concluded that this reflected a gender bias in the organization and that his supervisor was the lone exception. It was months before he learned that the women whom he felt were assigned less challenging work because they were women, were in fact all newly hired, junior researchers, and their work was what all junior researchers, female and male alike, were expected to do. What he attributed to gender was in fact a function of their lack of seniority in the organization. (There well may have been gender bias in the organization, but his observations in themselves should not have led to that conclusion.)

In the home, traditionally and still today, the woman manages the finances as well as matters of the schooling for children, if any, and other traditional responsibilities. Women with educational backgrounds comparable to their male classmates obtain comparable jobs in companies. If the woman marries and has children, she may leave the company for a period of several years, and then, in many cases, return—but without the seniority of the men she originally started with. There are fewer women in upper management, except in certain professions—fashion, for example—and this may be in part because of the glass ceiling. Japan has been criticized for the relatively small percentage of women executives and Diet (legislative) members compared to other modern societies, and this has been pointed out in reports on the status of women published by the United Nations. In the 1980s women in Japan were promised "equal opportunity" in the workplace, but experience has revealed a continued bias favoring male workers. One reason is that those making decisions about hiring assumed that most women would marry after a few years, have children, and leave the company. Then there is the possibility that, as a Japanese consultant says, a woman may look at the lives of her male counterparts in companies and think, "This is not the kind of life I want for myself" and make other choices. Given the perceived bias of companies toward men, many Japanese women say that they do not feel the same pressure to find a job with a good company and to stay with the company until retirement that many Japanese men feel, even as the expectation of lifetime employment, a given for men a generation ago, is no longer a safe assumption. Single women, in particular, may live at home while working, save some money, and travel overseas, study a foreign language, or pursue other interests. As a result, younger Japanese women often appear less conservative and more adventurous in their personal lives than do Japanese men of the same age and educational background.

Not surprisingly then, women and men who come from abroad to work in a Japanese organization often find understanding gender relations in the organization to be a challenge. A woman professional who goes to work in Japan is often accustomed to spending much time, often much more time, with men at work than with other women. In Japan there are times when there is no gender separation when working on projects, and it is not uncommon for the project manager to be female, supervising a largely male team. But as will be discussed later, lunchtime in the workplace often finds men and women sitting in separate areas of the company lunchroom, seemingly reflecting a pattern established during many years in school dining halls.

For women from abroad, gender relations after hours also take some getting used to. "In America, figuring out if it's okay to hang out with the boss is tricky." But about her experience of working in Japan, one woman said it was not unusual to go out with her boss to talk about future goals and plans, and even personal issues, adding "That kind of situation in the U.S. might be mistaken—that maybe she was trying to do something behind a person's back or having an affair." She said that at home she would probably avoid that situation or be very suspicious about something improper. "I cannot imagine having the same kind of relationships with an American boss."

Cultural values that affect how we judge relationships, especially those in which we have chosen to participate, appear in situations where there are gender matters and where one is sensitive that gender matters. Many expatriate employees, men as well as women, say they often feel more comfortable talking with Japanese women at work than with Japanese men. But women from abroad also feel uncomfortable in a Japanese organization when they find themselves only with other women, as is often the case at lunchtime. These are some of the reasons that Canadian consultant Gordon Jolley says, provocatively, that in Japanese companies today there are sometimes three genders: male, female, and *gaijin* (literally "foreigner," but primarily applied to people who are not from Asia). The relevance of gender and interpersonal relations that a Westerner may be accustomed to does not always fit the norm in a Japanese company. One former intern from the United States said she worked in the management division with her mostly male supervisors and that she had many opportunities to attend important business meetings with them and go out drinking after work, which she says she enjoyed. Yet at work she wore the same kind of uniform as other female workers who were in administrative positions. Lunchtime posed a problem: should she go to lunch with her female coworkers, or should she stay with her male supervisors? At first, it upset her that women and men did not mix the same way in Japan as they did in the U.S.

> Seriously, the social separation between men and women in Japan has been very frustrating personally and professionally. The majority of my U.S. friends are male, and it has been a new, but not unpleasant, experience to find myself in the company of women throughout most of each

day. Professionally, however, there are times when this separation reminds me of the U.S. "good old boy" system which has created the glass ceiling. Fortunately, I have found most managers less concerned with this phenomenon than with individual potential.

In the U.S. [male and female workers] are peers; they are on the same level and interact like that. Here they don't. They are either friends or the interaction clearly shows the difference between "office girls" and career guys. So because I'm a girl, I wear my uniform and I eat with girls in the cafeteria. I also became good friends with [male] managers. I do not mix with men often unless I met them somewhere [other than in her division], and then we are just friends. I don't get the same feeling that I'm doing things with men [without consciously thinking about their gender] in the United States.

Many women from overseas report that they feel also awkward going to lunch only with female workers and seeing that men and women do not mingle in ways in which they are accustomed. Whether working in an office or a lab, women say that their friends at work are almost always women. One woman from the U.S. said:

I don't know how women talk to each other but it's not the same thing as in America. In the U.S., they [male and female workers] are peers, you know, they are at the same level and interact like that. Here they don't. They are either friends or the interaction clearly shows the difference between "office girls" and career guys.

While the initial observations of expat men and women reflect their efforts to make sense of the work situation in which they find themselves, their descriptions and interpretations may also reveal a judgment about what they regard as fair and appropriate based on their own experience or expectations at home. Expressing such judgment to their Japanese coworkers may not be viewed favorably, however, even if their coworkers share that judgment.

An American woman who described the company she joined as conservative even by Japanese company standards wished she had a sense of more progressive work environments. She qualified her comments, recognizing her biases and that her experience was just one snapshot of Japanese corporate life. The women in her section, she said, were young and generally had less formal education than the male workers. She thought that the women in her division had no power and that she did not have any authority, either. As she saw it, the women in her section generally were expected to work, get married, and then quit.

21

When I first arrived here, I went on a tour of the plant. There was a section we walked by with all women working. The manager leading us on the tour told us that they could probably make the section more efficient by automating it, "but that would mean losing the women employees and the engineers do need wives." In fact, I hear half of our company's employees marry other employees. At first, I was offended. All my independent American bias made me think I was working for a company that did not really respect women. As I have been here longer and have seen women get married and then quit, or get married, get pregnant, and then quit, I began to realize that it is a choice. Many of the women I work with talk of how they want to get married and quit working. Even though those are not my life decisions, I cannot blame them for wanting to live their lives in that way. Nor can I blame a company for not wanting to invest much in women employees whom they rightfully assume will no longer work once married. However, I still believe it is too bad in some respects. Those women who are ambitious, who do want careers, really have no chance to advance either. For how could the company possibly tell the difference?

A young man from the U.S. who worked at a Japanese steel company described his early observations of five women who were in his section. At the time he thought the women were *"O.L."* (*ofisu redi*) literally "office ladies," a term commonly used by Japanese to indicate female office workers who do routine tasks without management responsibilities.

I have seen the following tasks performed: answering phones, reviewing technical documents, data entry, drafting forms, making copies, sending faxes, serving coffee and refreshments, emptying trash, and cleaning the kitchen area. I am sure that there are many other duties that they do. They usually work around nine hours a day, but I have seen some of them stay as late as 9:00 P.M. Every one I have asked has attended college. In my opinion they are a valuable asset to the office environment. As far as I know, they are well respected by the male office workers. There is a sexual harassment policy. There is also a family leave policy, where a woman may take leave for a year after giving birth.

Three months after he made these comments, he learned that the women were actually *kaishain* (regular employees). Two were architects and one worked in human resources.

The relationship between gender and one's self-identity as well as gender and roles within an organization is complex, changing, and sometimes conflicting within the values and hopes of an individual. Many young women consider marriage and having children as central to what they value, desire, and expect. Others place greater importance on self-fulfillment and contributing to society through professional achievements. Many want both, whether simultaneously or in some sequence.

For additional reading, we recommend Sumiko Iwao, *The Japanese Woman: Traditional Image and Changing Reality* (Harvard University Press, 1993), Dorrine Kondo, *Crafting Selves: Power, Gender, and Discourses of Identity in a Japanese Workplace* (University of Chicago Press, 1990), and Yuko Ogasawara, *Office Ladies and Salaried Men: Power, Gender, and Work in Japanese Companies* (University of California Press, 1998).

THREE

三

More than Meets the Eye: All About Context

When we hear the expression that something is taken out of context, we usually think of a larger verbal context. In Japan there are other contexts that must be considered to understand communication. This chapter describes some of these contexts.

KŪKI: SOMETHING IN "THE AIR"

The air or emotional atmosphere, vague but palpable feelings—these are central in the context of interpersonal relations and communication in Japan. To "read the air" and sense what others are thinking or feeling without having to ask is an art, a mark of maturity, and an essential quality of leadership and management. It is all about the value of sensing the immediate context—not just one occasion and relationships, but the mood that is indicated in myriad ways, nearly all unspoken. What recently happened that might be affecting how the people present are feeling and what they might be thinking, wondering about, or worried about? What are people thinking but not likely to say because they know others are thinking the same thing? Such questions are in the air, the *kūki* that we all try to read. This is a universal experience, but what is significant in Japan is the value of "reading the air" and not always needing or wanting things to "be spelled out," as in saying, "Let's clear the air" or "Let's get this out into the open." If a meeting has been called to consider an important decision, the manager or person in charge may decide to defer the decision if the kūki indicates it might be better to wait until later, after more informal discussion can make it easier to reach consensus.

K.Y. is a Japanese slang expression that emerged in the 1990s. K.Y.(*kūki ga yomenai*) refers to someone who, literally, "can't read the air," someone who doesn't get it, someone who is "clueless." K.Y. is one of those abbreviations created by a texting generation of Japanese that spread throughout the country. K.Y. might also describe the feelings of many Westerners who go to work in Japan—or anyone entering a new culture—but in Japan it refers to another Japanese who can't read the air. Sensing what is happening in relationships at the moment is important and foreshadows the future. The immediate context, the here and now one senses, affects all aspects of what is said, including how to interpret what one hears and how one considers what to say—or not say.

PLACE AS CONTEXT

Place is often an essential context of communication in Japan, so much so that people move from one place and time to another in order to have the conversation they want. It is more than a concern for privacy or other practical considerations. Often it is that how one interprets and responds to what is said in one setting is understood to convey a meaning that is different from what can be said in another. Examples of this, and reactions from some people unfamiliar with the culture, appear in the following text. There are settings and occasions that are chosen for getting to know one another that are different from an office setting where the same people meet and talk. Sometimes this may seem inefficient—"Can't we just discuss this on the phone?" one might wonder. But an e-mail, a phone call, a meeting at the office, or getting together for a meal are all different contexts and convey and allow for different things to be said and different goals to be reached.

An Australian bank manager who came to Japan described his feelings of puzzlement when Japanese colleagues from different banks were trying to decide what restaurant to meet at for a dinner meeting. When a Japanese colleague later told her all of the possible considerations regarding relationships, degree of seriousness of the occasion, what the place might suggest about the host and the guests, and much more, the newcomer from Melbourne was amazed. "I thought it was mostly about convenience, menu, and cost. Those considerations seemed the least of it!"

Technological changes and economic demands have had an impact in Japan as elsewhere. The *keitai* (cell phone) has altered connections in time and place. The once standard *"go-fun-mae-kōdō,"* meaning to be present at least five minutes before the scheduled time as a matter of manners and expression of respect remains important, especially for those from a pre-keitai generation. Famous places for meeting—the faithful dog Hachikō (the statue at Shibuya station in Tokyo which was *the* conventional meeting place in that area for generations)— mean less today than when people planned a time and place to meet and had no way to be in touch to revise their plans as is normal today. Still, the principle of place as a context for how to interpret words as well as one that fosters or constrains what might be said and conveys meaning in itself are all features of communication in Japan not to be underestimated.

SHARED KNOWLEDGE AND ASSUMPTIONS AS CONTEXT

"In America, words are the way to communicate; in Japan, words are *a* way to communicate." Masao Kunihiro, anthropologist, government advisor, and former Diet member, expressed simply what others have said in more elaborate ways, even in the form of a theory about words and all that provides the context for the words, that helps us interpret how to interpret the words, and that may indeed be even more important than the words themselves.

If all meaning were expressed in words taken at face value—where "yes" always meant yes, and "no" always meant no—then context could largely be ignored: it would matter not at all who said the "yes" or the "no," to whom, in what situation, and in what form—spoken or written—and if spoken in a soft voice or a shout. If relationships are clear and unalterable, if things never change, then words may carry a different kind of meaning.

In a traditional wedding ceremony, vows are exchanged; this is an essential part of the ceremony. But taken at face value, the promises exchanged are vague. Compare that with prenuptial agreements that are reviewed and formalized by attorneys: they include explicit enumeration of what is promised and what is not, and what will happen if conditions in the agreement are breached. Or compare a spoken promise affirmed with a handshake with something "in writing," dated and signed by the parties. There are matters where trust, reputation, or just gut feelings are sufficient for one to enter into an agreement with another. And there are matters where we want a precise statement, a written contract that we believe reduces ambiguity and minimizes misunderstandings for both parties. In most societies we experience and value both. The particular situations and application of these, however, differ across cultures.

In our lives, in our work, and in our relationships, paying attention to what someone says is often important, sometimes crucial. But it is not just the words said, but how they are said, who says them (and sometimes words that were expected but not said), where they are said, or how they are expressed—face to face, in an e-mail, in a voice message, and so on. All of those other parts of communication are often the most important part. Where relationships are irrelevant—for example, instructions on installing a computer program—what matters are words that are clear and that can be taken literally, at face value.

But we know that what gives meaning to our lives cannot easily be put into words.

The late American anthropologist Edward T. Hall pointed out in his theory of content that we can put our trust in words to understand and be understood, or we can look for meaning in the context within which the words are spoken— such as who says the words, where and how they are spoken, and so on. Cultures differ in what they emphasize. On a world scale, America ranks very high in the trust one puts in words and low in the importance of knowing the context as the carrier of meaning. Japan, and indeed much of the world, seems more comfortable in paying attention to context in order to interpret the meaning of words that may be said. The reasons for the difference are many, but some important reasons are clear. The better people know each other, the less that needs to be put explicitly in words.

Close family relations or friends of many years can often sense what the other is thinking without having to be told because they have shared so much that just a few words tap a reservoir of meaning. Strangers can assume little about what the other is thinking and thus have to rely on words. Where tradition or precedent is a reliable indicator, less new information may need to be expressed than in a new relationship where nothing can be taken for granted. Where people are heavily dependent on what others think, especially in the form of social pressure, maintaining one's reputation is crucial. This applies to other matters as well—contracts, for example. In cultures where context more than "in writing" is all that matters, a contract represents a kind of best guess, a formalized point in a changing reality, so that if the terms of a contract cannot be met, the parties will get together and discuss things again. Where words outweigh context, then the terms of a contract tend to be fixed and rigid. In a survey in Japan, people were asked what should be done if a contract had been signed but after a period of time it was impossible to fulfill the terms because conditions had changed. Less than a quarter of those surveyed responded that "a contract is a contract," and people should feel bound by its terms. Two-thirds chose the alternative—to talk it out with the other party and see what adjustments might be made.

Where sensitivity to "context" is important, the burden of understanding lies with the person hearing or reading, and if present, observing. Where there is less attention to the who, where, how, and when of the message—the "low context" manner of expression—the burden is on the person who wants to send the message.

Interculturalist Janet Bennett suggests a different metaphor: wide scanning or narrow scanning. Japanese, like many others—like most others in the world, perhaps—scan widely, observing and sensing one's place in relationships, occasion, hints, and more. The more familiar people are with the many contexts in which and with which they work, the more efficient interpersonal communication can be. "A word to the wise is sufficient" is said in the West, but it resonates in Japan.

Communication that is expressed and assumed to be understood without being said in so many words can be a source of anxiety for someone who expects an explicit verbal message, as in the case of "feedback" about one's performance at work. As we will discuss in Chapter 7, North Americans experience considerable stress if they do not receive the kind of explicit verbal feedback they expect. Even after a year's work in Japan some returned home, frustrated because there were not sure what their supervisor thought of their work.

Similarly, when a Japanese is hired by a Japanese company, he or she might not be given a precise job description; the new employee may not even know what the salary and benefits will be, a condition that few Westerners would feel comfortable with. "How do you know you will even get paid?" an American asked a Japanese friend who described this situation. The Westerner wants the promise stated clearly in words. The Japanese places the trust more in other matters—the company's reputation or the person who may have recommended the candidate.

DOUBLE STANDARDS

Anthropologist Chie Nakane was once quoted by a *Newsweek* reporter as saying "the Japanese have no principles." Taken out of context, that seems a terrible thing to say about any people.

Many people pride themselves on being people of principle, even if they do not always live up to those principles. They would like the same principles to apply to all people in all situations. Experience may not conform to these ideals. Japanese communication, as noted, values sensitivity to situations, to doing or saying what is appropriate in a particular circumstance. The Japanese do not expect all people to be treated in the same way in all situations, nor do they think it is wise to always say what one believes. From a Japanese point of view this is a recognition that a "case by case" practicality should be regarded as necessary and practical. ("Case-by-case" is an idiom often used in Japan, in English.)

TATEMAE AND HONNE

Many who study about Japan have heard the Japanese terms *tatemae* and *honne* to describe two standards that work in parallel, not in conflict. Tatemae is literally the outward structure of a building; the term refers to what is outwardly expressed, what appears on the surface ("façade" conveys the wrong impression). It is the appropriate presence. Honne, literally one's "true voice," refers to what one really thinks or feels. The Japanese assume that there may be a difference between what one says and what one thinks. How else could it be in a society that values harmony in interpersonal relations, that discourages individualistic outspokenness, and that restrains the bold expression of personal feelings? It is not that this is unique to Japan: everywhere one recognizes the voice that says, "This is what we say, but let's be honest (or practical)."

The effects of this difference in "standards" are many. Japanese are more likely to take into account the circumstances in which something is expressed and judge accordingly how much reflects honne and how much is tatemae. Context is all-important. Westerners who expect to be able to take words at face value and discover a difference between what someone says and what is actually believed may be upset and complain. A German reporter living in Japan once defined "honne" as "duplicity." Japanese, on the other hand, may sympathize with a person who is put into a situation where it is difficult for that person to say what he or she is thinking.

Those who go to work in Japan are well advised to always consider the circumstances in which something is said. While this may also be good advice everywhere, the occasions, settings, and "contexts" in Japan generally exert much more influence on what is said or not said than is the case for many Westerners. Often circumstances dictate whether one can reveal one's "true voice," or say what is expected or what circumstances constrain one to say. One's true voice can be heard in a situation that allows for it. This is one reason the informal, after-hours settings for gathering with coworkers are so important in Japan. For the same reasons, foreigners working with Japanese should take care not to ask blunt questions in situations where the Japanese would find it difficult to respond frankly.

Expats working in Japan have complained that they get "too much tatemae" from the Japanese and not enough honne. Said one expatriate manager with considerable overseas experience and who is now based in Osaka, "It's a lot harder to know what my Japanese staff members are thinking than with people from any other culture I've worked with." Japanese, on the other hand, are sometimes irked by what they feel is childish, to express a "true voice" in situations where more tatemae is called for—as in some formal settings or in staff sessions with the top officials of the organization.

But there is more to this than an imbalance of courtesy and candor. There is a kind of American style of tatemae that Japanese sometimes interpret as honne. A Japanese engineer, transferred to the American home office, was at first confused and then upset when Americans, seeming outwardly so friendly, would make vague overtures of invitations to dinner but never follow through. Later he philosophized, "Americans think we Japanese are too polite for too long—but it takes a longer time for Japanese to become real friends. But Americans, I think, seem too friendly too soon, so we Japanese don't know if they are really friendly or just being polite American style."

CONTEXT AND RECIPROCITY

There is a context of a social balance sheet, in matters small and large. In New York, "I owe you lunch!" may be a joke about the next time friends will meet. In Japan the calculation of social reciprocity may be more serious. One feature of interpersonal relations in Japan can be likened to what happens on a seesaw, when one of the people moves up on the board in such a way as to cause the other to be elevated, and the other end tips down to the ground. Was it the lowering that caused the other to rise, or allowing the other to rise that caused oneself to be lowered? Or is it that these are both part of the same process? Japanese show respect and express gratitude and politeness by elevating, in words and actions, the other person. Like the physics of the seesaw, they can do the same by humbling themselves. Both the deference that raises the other and the humility that humbles oneself are basic principles of interpersonal relations in Japan. Indeed, the logic of the seesaw is sometimes almost comical when two people attempt to out-humble themselves or out-compliment the other. Westerners may do as well as the Japanese in extolling praise for or expressing concern about the other, but they may not be as prepared to be quite as self-effacing as their Japanese friends.

In the implicit hierarchy in Japanese relations, where one is always conscious of who defers to whom, there is little ambiguity about the meaning of polite amenities. Often the conversation simply reaffirms a relationship, treating a person as he or she expects or feels entitled to be treated. When this is lacking, the person may be irritated or confused. The same thing sometimes happens in other societies of course. When customers feel they are not being treated courteously by salespeople in a store, or when parents feel they are not shown some modicum of respect from their offspring, they are bothered or feel hurt. In the army that sort of thing is called insubordination. American culture in particular, however, discourages people from expecting any special treatment that has not been "earned." The expectation of being treated in a certain way by virtue of one's relationship with another is the norm in Japan. One does not expect to have to negotiate each new relationship. Thus it is that Japanese managers in factories can dress like everybody else and eat in the company cafeteria alongside the workers without feeling that their position is threatened: everybody knows the relationship without its having to be demonstrated outwardly.

While who sits where and who defers to whom will be perfectly clear within an organization where people know each other, what happens when strangers meet? How does one know how to act appropriately? Several points should be noted.

First of all, Japanese do not always know how to tip that seesaw when they first meet someone, particularly if the meeting is informal and unexpected and if there is no clear difference in age. They may ask some of the same questions anyone would in the same situation, but do so more cautiously and with an ear to learning at least who is older. In business and professional circles, *meishi* (business cards) will be exchanged, and the recipients will pay most attention to the other's position in the company. Companies or other organizations, of course, also have their own status and relative rank, just as they do anywhere, and this too enters into the calculation.

Japanese do their homework in preparing for meetings with others. There may be cultural differences in how one thinks of when communication begins: at the time of the actual, physical meeting of people, or long before with messages exchanged and homework done to know whom one will be meeting. The Japanese will want to know at least enough about the person he is meeting for the first time in order to act appropriately, rather than trying to figure out the relationship at the time of the meeting. All this has to do with more than just *aisatsu* (greetings), of course, for it also anticipates what kind of future relationship, if any, should be encouraged. This desire to be prepared for meetings is one reason Japanese prefer to use an intermediary in making introductions, for the third party can help to clarify a situation in a way that avoids awkwardness and potential embarrassment. It is also a reason that Japanese are uncomfortable with "cold calls" from persons who want to do business. Businesspeople who arrive at a Japanese company without warning do not make a good impression and are not likely to be well received. The company is literally unprepared to receive them.

NEGOTIATING STYLES

The importance of context and the expectation of reciprocity are both central to Japanese negotiating styles, as explained by United Nations University Vice Rector and international relations professor Kinhide Mushakoji's distinction between the adjusting style (*awase*) and the selecting style (*erabi*). Does one first try to create a social context of relationships and then see what is possible, or does one begin with a plan of demands: business before pleasure?

The erabi style is that of a choicemaker, one who chooses or selects—the style associated with American negotiators. On the assumption that one has some control over events and that one enters into a bargaining situation only when one's goal is clear, the erabi style is marked by a series of choices that lead directly to the desired goal. In presenting his theory, Mushakoji notes that these choices are of an "either/or" and "yes or no" sort; he compares them with the kind of choices one makes when playing chess. For instance, Americans who speak about their "game plan" clearly exemplify the erabi way of thinking.

The awase style, on the other hand, is characterized by continuous adjustment to an ever-changing environment. "Awase" comes from the word *awaseru*, meaning to adjust to something else or to combine; this is the style associated with the Japanese. From an awase point of view, one cannot proceed toward a fixed goal but rather must adjust to changing and uncertain conditions. The awase-style negotiator, therefore, may not have a fixed goal in mind until after entering into negotiations and sensing what might be possible under the circumstances. Consistent with this, the language of awase style is "more-or-less" rather than "either-or." Nuance and shades of meaning are very important.

A television set provides an analogy for the two kinds of negotiating styles. The erabi or American style is likened to choosing one channel or another. The awase style is more like the volume control, which may be adjusted to be slightly softer or a little louder, depending on circumstances.

What happens when more traditional Japanese and Westerners attempt to negotiate and the awase and erabi styles meet? In the first place, there may be a clash of protocols. One side may want to put forth their proposals immediately, to "lay their cards out on the table"—again the game metaphor is revealing. The Japanese may not be prepared to do so; they may want to spend much more time during which, in effect, they can come to know the other side better so as to see what might be worked out. Thus the one side may be viewed as too "fast," too blunt or aggressive, and possibly too uncompromising. The other side, in contrast, may be perceived as too "slow," too cautious, and too guarded about their position.

The awase-style negotiator also assumes that the adjustments will be reciprocal, though the expectation of a quid pro quo may not be stated. Americans do not make this same assumption. There are many cases in business and government relations where the Japanese have been startled to find that Americans did not reciprocate as expected.

The awase (Japanese) mode of thinking also expects there to be an unavoidable gap between form and reality: "We say things should be this way but we know that in practice it is not so simple." This is very different from the erabi style, which usually is most concerned about the formal outcome of negotiations—the agreement, contract, or whatever. If one side wants to have detailed and binding contracts while the Japanese would prefer a less precise document that serves as a symbol of their efforts to work together, there may be problems. Japanese may continue to negotiate for favors after a contract has been signed, a position that those accustomed to the erabi mode regard as most improper.

The erabi/awase comparison like others, such as the role of context, can be overdrawn and in an ever-changing, globally connected world, suggest contrasts that are less apparent in the early 21st century than they were a decade or two earlier. And yet these distinctions have value as points of reference, an expanded perspective about intercultural communication. To state a choice and await the other's response, or to be more cautious and want to sense the other's feelings and preferences before proceeding—this distinction continues to be one that is helpful when working in Japan.

FOUR

Everyday Communication

"Communication" as a word has a relatively short history, and is novel enough to be a foreign word borrowed into Japanese. But what that word identifies is as old as human history—older, actually. The European tradition is to identify "communication" with the spoken word, and historically at least back to Aristotle and the beginning of "the liberal arts" which featured the artful use of words (Rhetoric) as fundamental. We know now that our words convey a relatively small part of our communication.

FIRST AND LASTING IMPRESSIONS

Though fashion changes from year to year, and in Japan varies a bit from region to region—professional women in the Kansai area (including Osaka and Kobe) prefer brighter colors than their counterparts in the more somber Kanto area (including Tokyo and Yokohama)—two features of attire and appearance are constant: neatness and cleanliness. Not just first impressions but all interpersonal communication begins with the visual, beginning with well-shined shoes.

In Japanese bookstores and online there are many manuals that advise the new employee on the dress code and manners expected in most companies, although some of the dress codes and manners have been relaxed in recent years. Individual companies also have their own policies regarding appearance. The dress code covers all aspects of appearance: what to wear, hair, nails, and even bags and shoes. In more conservative companies, women will be advised on hair color and length, and men will be advised on hair length, including the length of sideburns, and facial hair.

The contrast between Japanese college students' clothing and grooming during the first three years of school and during the fourth year, which is when students often absent themselves from classes to seek employment and attend job interviews, is remarkable.

Japanese young people who are job hunting often go through a major transformation in appearance, including changes in hair style, hair coloring (returning to dark brown or black if their hair had been dyed), and even in posture. Some students report that their posture automatically changes when they don the standard "recruit uniform." Moving from student life to work life can seem difficult as adapting to a foreign culture, even for those who have grown up in Japan.

Every year clothing companies, department stores, and often university co-op shops promote the sale of suits and accessories that are appropriate for the rounds of job interviews that students undertake, typically from their third year of college. Along with the selection of a suit may be advice on grooming and other personal matters that can affect one's success in being invited to join a company. Shoes should be standard, always shined, with heels in good shape, and worn with appropriate socks or stockings. Men's pants should be well pressed, and women's clothes should be appropriate for their role and occasion, with coordinated accessories.

We should note that being appropriately attired is only a first consideration. One's comportment is even more important.

A study of job interviews by college students revealed differences between Japanese and U.S. students who were fluent in Japanese. Several of the U.S. students crossed their legs while being interviewed, while no Japanese students did—crossing one's legs in the presence of someone who is older or in a higher status position is considered impolite in Japan

From the perspective of a visitor, dress for Japanese workers looks standardized, especially for those who are newly employed. But within this uniformity there are individual variations that those within the group will express and notice. Moreover, even within a general uniformity of clothing there may be some variations that puzzle the newcomer. Why do some women wear more fashionable clothes than others? Why can some women wear more casual dresses while most others are in suits? The differences may be because the people in the office are from different divisions, or under different kinds of contracts (full time, temp worker, and so on), and sometimes differing because of age and number of years in the organization. For someone coming from abroad to work in Japan, the advice is to start off by dressing conservatively, observe what others are wearing, and adjust accordingly. For the newly arrived intern or employee from abroad, the standard advice is to look to the newest employees as exemplifying—or trying to—company policy.

In 2005, with the increased concern for saving energy, Prime Minister Junichiro Koizumi encouraged a new summer dress code that would reduce the use of air conditioning in offices. If men were not wearing suits in the office, the temperature would not need to be set so low. Many women also appreciated the proposal because while the men in suits may have been comfortable, women often felt chilly. Thus began the practical encouragement for what is called "cool biz," which could include traditional Okinawan shirts, or dress shirts without coat and tie. Some offices have adopted the fashion, but it has caused some social discomfort, such as when a younger person in the "cool biz" style meets a senior person who is wearing a coat and tie.

Clothing in Japan reflects the individual's relationship to the group much more than is so in the West. Japan has been called a nation of uniforms, not just for mail carriers, clerks, and clergy, but also for students, housewives, businesspeople, entertainers, and vacationers. (Guests who stay at a hot springs resort will don the hotel's *yukata*, the lightweight cotton kimono, so that even while strolling about town, others can immediately identify who is staying at which resort hotel.)

Most of these uniforms are by no means official, but it is not so difficult for an alert Japanese to pick out on a crowded commuter train who is who on the basis of how each is dressed. Many companies have standard dress policies or uniforms. At the Sony offices and plants in Japan there is a standard smock that everybody, factory worker and president alike, wears. At Sony's large plant in San Diego, on the other hand, American employees objected to having to dress alike at work, so the company gave up the dress code at that location.

Commuting to and from work, employees are also regarded as representing their organization. This means that in some companies even if one keeps a uniform in a locker at work, it is not acceptable for the employee to commute wearing jeans and then change at work. Typically, during a company's entrance ceremony and orientation programs, new employees will be told, "You will now be representing our company and we expect behavior that reflects well on our company's policy at all times."

Neatness and cleanliness are the most important criteria. Fashions of hair length for men will change, but even when longer hair is the norm, when considering cleanliness as the guide, hair trimmed above the collar for men is standard. Women who have long hair will tie back their hair if it covers their face or when working in the office if it touches the desk.

In our study of North Americans working in Japan, one of the interns was a Native American whose long hair was an expression of his identity, not a matter of personal preference. When his supervisor, concerned that the intern's hair length could be an issue in the company, asked him if he wanted to have a haircut, the intern explained that the long hair was important as an expression of his cultural heritage. The supervisor looked into the company's regulations and found that there was no specific reference to men's length of hair, but still the supervisor knew that the directors and other top-level managers didn't like men having long hair. Nevertheless, she sided with the intern and helped upper management understand this special situation, and the intern enjoyed a very successful internship. (The supervisor told the authors that it became a nonissue; she laughed that the only time others were reminded of it was during a company excursion to a hot springs inn and the intern needed a little more time to dry and comb his hair.)

IN A MANNER OF SPEAKING

1. The Line and the Curve: Directness and Indirectness

Conversational styles differ, one might say, geometrically. One preference in "serious discussions" is for the linear—lines of argument, lines of reasoning. "The bottom line" has moved from the accountant's ledger to refer to any "baseline" principle. These lines move to points: to come to the point and make several points when discussing something. Lines and points. In contrast, a feature of Japanese communication may favor the curve. To go around something rather than "straight to the point" is preferred. Points stick out. Points might injure someone. In Japan, one takes care to avoid either eventuality. English speakers grow up with a whole set of negative expressions about the circular: "going around in circles," "beating around the bush," and the like. A circular style suggests vague thinking or a fear of saying what one really means, and it may also seem time-consuming, inefficient.

For example, if someone in Boston needs a ride to the airport he or she might say to a friend, "I hesitate to ask, but I have an early flight tomorrow morning and need a ride to the airport. Would you be able to take me?" In Sapporo might be more like: "I have to get up early tomorrow morning—I have an early flight"—and then wait for the friend to respond, "Do you need a ride?" And if the friend in Boston can't offer a ride, he or she might say, "I'm sorry I can't help you, but . . ." and then provide a reason. In the same situation in Sapporo, the friend who gets the hint may express sympathy and may also give a reason but would not say, "I can't help you." Both the person asking the favor and the other understand the situation and neither has asked or declined directly.

From the Japanese perspective, being direct and to the point can mean being insensitive to the other's feelings as well as lacking in aesthetic subtlety, at least in the setting of a formal business meeting. In other settings, Japanese can be more direct about some matters than the Americans. A Japanese professional interpreter says:

> Americans can be just as indirect as the Japanese, but they are indirect about different things, and being indirect carries a different meaning. Americans are usually indirect when something very sensitive is being discussed or when they are nervous about how the other person might react. Whenever Americans are indirect, I suspect that something is going on!
>
> Japanese indirectness is a part of our way of life. It is not because we are such kind and considerate people that we worry so about the other's reactions. It is just that we know that our own fates and fortunes are always bound up with others. I think you can value directness when you value individualism, or when you are with people you know and trust completely.

When the interpreter was asked how the Japanese perceived American directness, she said this:

> It depends on the situation, of course. We're more direct about some things than many Americans, who retain some Victorian language habits even though they might not think so. But generally we associate the American sort of directness with the expression of power or authority within a group, like a general barking out commands. We do that too, maybe even more than Americans, within our group—that is, the boss can do that. It's when somebody talks that way to people who are equals or not well known that it is a problem.

In the place where one is a part of the group—family or company—there can also be a directness that shocks outsiders who imagine that everything in Japan is all indirect and kind. Bosses can be so direct to the point of seeming cruel by some Western standards. Where the hierarchy is strict, and especially across generations, there can be a directness rarely seen or tolerated in "the West." In the Japanese legislature, disputes that in London or Washington

would be concealed in a gauze of politeness one associates with Japanese nice-
ties can burst into virtual—and real—fights that are cause for international
news stories.

Richard Harris, a Londoner who has taught (in Japanese) for three decades
in the Department of International Business at Chukyo University, has remarked
on increasing directness he has observed in Japan.

> Indirectness is often conspicuous by its absence in many encounters I
> have here, and I think it is fairly general. My wife and I recently went into
> a coffee shop we had not been to for a while, and the minute we walked in
> the master (whom we do not know well) greeted us with "You must have
> been back to the U.S. Did you bring me a present?" I hear Japanese friends
> talking to each other with similar directness. Modesty also seems to be less
> of a virtue, but then again I work in academia, where it has never been a
> professional characteristic.

2. The Go-Between

When hoping to meet someone for the first time and sometimes when conveying
a difficult or delicate message, the Japanese find that the use of a third party, or
go-between, can be most effective. Even a note with one's business card introduc-
ing one person to another can be an appropriate proxy. As mentioned earlier,
when the kindergarten teacher mentioned in Chapter 1 acted as a buffer between
the children in the class and the visitors, she did so for at least two reasons: for
one, she was the *sekininsha*, the responsible person in the situation; second,
she served a basic function of a go-between: to deflect direct contact between
people who might find it awkward, confusing, or disruptive. In any enterprise
of importance, be it a marriage or a business venture, the go-between in Japan
plays a prominent role. He or she provides background information for both
parties, attempts to set the right mood for the first meeting, and ensures that
the parties are serious and sincere. If things do not go well, then the go-between
can soften the bad news and lessen the disappointment. If a union is made, then
the go-between remains a human bond in the contract. To dissolve that union,
whether a marriage or a business partnership, also involves the go-between, and
thus there is extra pressure for people to resolve disputes.

No doubt people in every society also use contacts, third parties as media-
tors, and such, but in many Western societies the preference is often for more
direct contact. (As the teachers in the American kindergartens told the visiting
researchers, "Go ahead and tell the kids what you want them to do.") In working with the Japanese, outsiders often appear too direct: they are likely to leave

out the middleman or fail to go through the proper channels. Sometimes this is because Westerners in Japan do not know who to involve or how to proceed. In many cases, however, there is a cultural reason for wanting to get on with things and not waste time. As it so often turns out, however, the direct approach in Japan is the least efficient. In Japan, often the shortest distance between two points is a curved line.

There is one kind of third party that the Japanese have used less frequently than in many other modern societies: the lawyer. The lawyer's role, in fact, is partly to aid clarity and reduce some ambiguities by putting things in writing in a language that should make it clear where each side stands. American contracts are usually very detailed and make explicit agreements, intentions, and consequences. Japanese contracts seem by comparison to be general and vague. The U.S. also has many times the number of lawyers that Japan has, at least partly because Japanese disputes are usually settled out of court. The lawyer's role has increased in Japan in the past decades, but in many cases a lawyer will be called in only when problems have reached a crisis stage. "When a lawyer shows up," a perceptive observer once remarked, "it is like the appearance of a Buddhist priest who is called in to administer the last rites." With globalization, the presence and role of the lawyer has increased dramatically in Japan, but mostly at the level of the company or other organization. That a commonplace dispute might escalate into a legal challenge is not what comes to mind. Challenges to abusive practices by companies in Japan have made people more sensitive to these important options, but for now the traditional concerns are more apparent. Unfortunately, this has also made it possible for the criminal elements to exploit the most vulnerable in Japan.

3. Beginnings and Endings

Another visible expression of harmony in the Japanese kindergarten was the way the children began and concluded their work together. To start before others or to turn in one's work while others are still working sets one apart. It may also suggest that the person is rude, selfish, or not well-brought-up. Such an attitude is not unknown to Americans, but Americans are more likely to associate beginning and ending as a group with a formal occasion, such as a religious service or formal dinner. And Americans say they prefer informality.

Japanese have many everyday expressions to announce the beginning and ending of activities. There are set expressions in Japanese for when one leaves the house and when one returns, when one begins a meal and when one is finished. Bus drivers may announce when the bus is starting and when it is stopping, and television news announcers will state that the program has begun and that it has come to an end. Such expressions always relate the individual to the group or help synchronize group activities. Department stores begin each day with a formal opening: chimes ring out, uniformed attendants swing open the doors, and the personnel in every section bow to the first arriving customers and bid them welcome. At closing time, it is the tune of *Auld Lang Syne* that announces the store is closing.

Group synchrony is enhanced in other ways, too—frequent meetings at work, dining and drinking with coworkers after hours, college dorm meetings. Sometimes Americans regard these as "ritualistic" and hence a waste of time. American students studying in Japan have been known to stop attending dorm or club meetings or come but then leave early because they have a test to study for or a paper to complete. Japanese students regard such behavior as selfish or "too individualistic." The same kind of behavior and judgment sometimes can be seen in tour groups when some people, not wanting to have to do what everyone else does, choose to go off on their own. When this happens in Japan, there can be problems. It is only common sense and common courtesy to first check with the guide.

One scene of coordination that sometimes can be glimpsed even by the casual visitor is the *chōrei*, or morning meeting. In some organizations this might be held only at the beginning of the week, and at others—at department stores, for example—people who will be working together hold coordinating meetings each morning to make sure that everyone is familiar with plans, goals, and any new information that must be shared.

Coordination can also be observed each morning in factory yards, schools, and sometimes on the street in front of shops and even high above the ground in modern office buildings. This is the sight of Japanese doing group calisthenics. "Ichi, ni, san, shi . . ." the radio exercise instructor calls out to the familiar radio exercise tune, as everybody bends and stretches in synchrony.

Communication research reveals that all people who collaborate, in work or even in ordinary conversation, unconsciously move toward ways of acting in synchrony. The stronger the relationship, the more apparent the synchrony. Where group solidarity and harmonious collaboration is most valued, conscious choices to foster synchrony are most likely to be found in ways large and small. When enjoying lunch with friends or coworkers, there is a tacit coordination of starting and finishing the meal together. And this is also found in the many ritual events that mark the shape of a year in Japan—most dramatically, in the movement of the people who shoulder the massive *omikoshi* (palanquins) during the multitude of Japanese festivals.

4. The Way

In the behavior observed in Japanese kindergartens, the Japanese teacher's direct guidance of the child's drawing, in contrast to the American's encouragement to "draw your picture the way you want it," suggests another important part of Japanese life: learning the proper form.

The suffix *-dō*, as in *judō*, *kendō*, and *bushidō*, means "the way," but the idea of a correct "way" extends far beyond traditional martial arts, *kadō*, (flower arrangement) and *shodō*, calligraphy in Japan for example. There is a right way to exchange condolences, a right way to greet one's superior, a right way to greet the New Year, and a right way to offer a drink, accept a gift, and decline a compliment. The way to learn the way, of course, is to be taught by those who are older and wiser, more experienced. One's elders and superiors command respect in part because they know a lot.

Take the example of the *meishi* (business card) exchange, an act performed maybe a million times every day in Japan. Because the card represents one's organization, the cards must be exchanged with all due respect. One receives another's card as one might a token gift, with thanks and appreciation. One should look at the card carefully and perhaps make some comment that serves to acknowledge receiving it. The card will then be carefully put aside for future reference; after the other party leaves, the recipient may write a note with the card to help remember something about the meeting in the future. (Most Japanese will keep these cards in a special file just for such purposes.) When presented, the cards are not to be dealt out like playing cards on a table or received and stuffed into a wallet and sat upon. The visitor who handles a card with little respect presents a poor image personally and of the organization that chose to hire him.

This does not mean that the Japanese expect foreigners to try to act like the Japanese. On the contrary: in Japan, the "strange foreigner," the *hen na gaijin*, is one who overdoes things, who tries, by Japanese standards, to "go native." A Japanese business consultant gave this advice:

> There are many things you should try to do properly when you are in Japan, but the Japanese do not expect you to do everything we do. You should try to know what the Japanese regard as the proper way, and then adjust accordingly.

5. "No" Ways

In her comparative research, Professor Mayumi Kubota concluded that Japanese people in conversation nod more frequently than any other society observed, and more than twice as frequently as people in the U.S. Westerners unfamiliar with Japan often mistake the nodding for agreement when it most often simply signals that one is listening. Some Japanese report feeling insecure when talking with someone who does not nod. Chinese students who are learning the Japanese language in China view videotapes rather than only audio recordings of conversations in order to develop the habit of nodding when speaking Japanese.

Even though the nod does not mean agreement, there is something affirming about the nod, for the Japanese are reluctant, in social conversation, to say "no" directly. In a famous study, researcher Keiko Ueda investigated some of the ways Japanese convey a "no" in situations, such as turning down a request. She identified sixteen different ways, including tangential responses, an apology, a conditional "yes," and silence. Though the equivalent of "no" (*iie*) is used in filling out forms and other such contexts, conversationally it sounds rude to respond with a sentence that begins with *iie*. Thus rather than replying to an inquiry about finding a time to meet as an English speaker might—"No, I can't meet you on Friday,"—a more indirect response such as "That might be difficult" is what is more likely to be said. Japanese management consultant Masaaki Imai borrowed the title of Ueda's study for his book on intercultural relations in business: *Sixteen Ways to Avoid Saying "No."* It was a follow-up to his earlier book with a delightful title that makes a similar point: *Never Take "Yes" for an Answer.* The signaling a negative without directly saying so is a particular example of the more general theme of higher context messages discussed in the previous chapter. Generally, when a Japanese manager responds to a suggestion or request with a remark like, "Hmmm, that might be difficult," or "Let me think about that," most likely another Japanese would take this as a fairly strong indication the answer is "no." Someone from outside of Japan who is unfamiliar with that contextual coding might well hold out hope for a "yes."

As the Japanese public was becoming more concerned about ecological issues, a convenience store chain thought about how to reduce the excessive use of plastic bags for even the smallest purchase. Aware that asking customers a question like, "Do you need a bag for this?" could create some discomfort for customers who would have to pause and then say "no," the store decided to ask the question in such a way that the customer could answer, "Yes." Both customer and clerk were happy

6. Speech Is Silver, but . . .

Most Americans are familiar with the expression "Silence is golden," but few know it in its most familiar form in Japan: "Speech is silver, but silence is golden." Indeed, Japanese proverbs indicating distrust of words and the value of silence are numerous. "Hollow drums make the most noise" is a favorite. In conversation, speaking too much may suggest immaturity or a kind of empty-headedness.

Americans tend to believe that if something hasn't been put into words it has not been communicated, and that if someone has something to say, he or she should say it. Studies show that American children are encouraged to speak more and do, indeed, speak more than do Japanese children of the same age at home and at school. Speaking or "speaking up" indicates for Americans a person who is paying attention, who has ideas, opinions, or information. Though everybody knows people who seem to talk too much, the greater concern of Americans is more likely to be that they do not speak up or speak out enough.

Conversely, Americans usually associate silence in social situations with something negative—tension, hostility, awkwardness, or shyness. And, although Americans in some situations clearly associate speaking with authority ("Let me do the talking"), both experience and folklore supply numerous examples of the little man who spoke out and whose words carried the day.

The Japanese attitudes toward speech and silence are quite different. Speaking in itself is not regarded as highly as it is in the West generally. A Japanese is hard put to think of any "great speeches" or even ringing quotations of Japanese speakers. Writing, however, holds enormous prestige.

Silences, on the other hand, have many meanings in a Japanese setting. Silence is not simply the absence of sound or speech, a void to be filled, as Americans tend to regard it. Not speaking can sometimes convey respect for the person who has spoken or the ideas expressed. Silence can be a medium that the parties share, a means of unifying, in contrast to words that separate. Silence in conversations is often compared to the white space in brush paintings or calligraphy scrolls. A picture is not richer, more accurate, or more complete if such spaces are filled in. To do so would be to confuse and detract from what is presented.

Japanese and Americans often confuse each other in the way they speak and treat silence. An American asks a Japanese a question and there is a pause before the Japanese responds. If the question is fairly direct, the pause may be even longer as the Japanese considers how to avoid a direct answer. The American, however, may assume that the pause is because the question was not clearly understood and hence he may rephrase the question. It often happens that the American is himself just uncomfortable with the silence and is trying to fill it with words to reduce his own uneasiness. In any case, the additional verbalization is only likely to make the situation more difficult for the Japanese. Not only has the American asked two or more questions in the space appropriate for one, he has separated himself by not sharing in a thoughtful silence. One observes this in classrooms and at public meetings where a visiting speaker invites questions after concluding a speech and interprets a silence as an awkward pause and so begins to talk some more.

Japan's feudal history has influenced current day attitudes toward speaking and keeping silent. To fit in was to know one's place; to speak out might well mean to lose one's head. Along with so many other features of Japanese society, attitudes toward speaking have changed considerably; older people complain that younger people talk too much these days. Listening respectfully is an appropriate behavior for one in a subordinate position—that is, one who is younger, of lower rank, serving as host, and so on. While this pattern has its counterparts in America, age, seniority, rank, and role as host or guest are not nearly as influential as in Japan. An American supervisor may admire an employee who speaks right up—depending upon what the person has to say. In Japan, it is more likely that the "speaking right up" in itself would be offensive. The American bright young man becomes the brash young man in Japanese terms.

A top American executive based in Tokyo discovered after working in Japan for several years that he had been misjudging Japanese associates by evaluating them largely on the basis of their styles of listening and speaking. "I just didn't realize that I had been taking quick, clear, direct questions as a sign of an alert listener and a good staff member. I wonder how many Japanese I have misjudged, in and out of the office, simply because they didn't give me that kind of response. Now I wonder if I hired the worst—least typically Japanese—and dismissed some of the best."

7. Your Most Enchanted Listener

Years ago the semanticist Wendell Johnson wrote a widely read book called *Your Most Enchanted Listener*. What Johnson had in mind was that we are our most enchanted listeners when we talk. The title came to mind when visiting with a Japanese friend who had studied in the United States and who had been living for a number of years in Honolulu. "There is one habit of Americans I still have not gotten used to," she said, "and it bothers me most when I come back here from being in Japan. The difference is so obvious: Japanese talk about each other, and Americans love to talk about themselves."

She explained, "If I tell a Japanese friend that I was just in Los Angeles, my friend will ask me what I saw, how I liked it, and so on. But if I tell an American the same thing, he will say, 'Oh, Los Angeles? I've got a cousin who lives in Long Beach. I've never been there. I really like L.A., and when I went shopping there last year . . . ' It's really irritating the way some people feel they can just turn the conversation to talk about themselves if they want to." The Japanese conscious-ness of the other person—the interdependent concern—stands in sharp contrast to Americans' more independent or individualistic focus. Not surprisingly, this is reflected in the communication styles of the two peoples and in their evalu-ations of each other.

The difference in orientations is apparent when friends who have not seen each other for a while happen to meet. Americans are likely to ask about each other and tell each other about where they have been or what they have been doing. Who speaks first does not seem to matter very much. When Japanese friends meet, one is likely to begin by thanking the other for some previous favor, gift, or letter that was sent. Most often, a reference to the last time they were together is part of this greeting. Thus they reestablish a context that frames their continuing relationship.

Westerners sometimes misinterpret the Japanese custom of expressing thanks or inquiring about some past event as "overdoing it." It also may embar-rass Westerners for, as one American said, "The Japanese always find something to thank me for before I can come up with something to thank them for. I sometimes think it's a kind of one-upmanship." The interpretation of thanking as a kind of game is actually not very helpful here. The desire to begin by refer-ring to something that relates the parties, as mentioned, is one factor. Another reason is the genuine uneasiness Japanese occasionally feel about being in social debt; better to err on the side of excessive politeness than to be insuf-ficiently polite. (Ill-mannered behavior, remember, reflects poorly not only on the individual but on the family, school, or company of which the person is a part.) A third reason is that this is the proper form, and doing what is expected is very important.

9. Modesty and Politeness

Modesty is a virtue, a social grace, in most societies. A boastful, self-centered person is as tedious in Sydney as in Sapporo. Japanese and Westerners alike appreciate a hero who brushes off words of praise for his or her actions. There are, however, some differences.

As a rule, Americans can risk sounding "overly modest" by American stan-dards and still be well within the realm of "appropriately modest" by Japanese standards. A more important rule is to resist speaking about oneself or one's achievements in ways that are self-promoting. While there is something in Ameri-can culture that allows or even encourages a person to "sell yourself," the notion of merchandising oneself does not sit well with the Japanese, who generally do not like to stand out or be singled out, even by others, and it is considered far worse to promote oneself.

Describing the difference in terms of Eastern and Western values generally, a Chinese journalist in Japan recalled the heroes in the martial arts movies, like the Kung Fu films: "You'll notice that Bruce Lee never shows how good he is until he has to act. Only the bad guys and the unskilled show off. That's not just part of the Bruce Lee character, that's an Asian virtue." Among the proverbs one hears quoted the most when Japanese talk about Japanese values (particularly in contrast to Western values) is: "The clever hawk hides its claws."

The expression of modesty is apparent in a variety of situations. A telling difference can be found in a study of personal ads in the classified ads in some Japanese publications, which are similar to those that appear in big cities elsewhere. While it wouldn't be unusual for an American ad to begin, "Attractive, athletic, male with a good sense of humor seeks . . . ," a comparable Japanese ad might start out with "Though I am not very good looking . . . "

When one offers something to another person, such as a gift or a meal that one has prepared, the same kind of depreciation is called for in Japan. There are set expressions for such humility: "It's nothing" or "It's nothing special." Never take such apologies at face value. The hostess who apologizes to her guests that "There is nothing (special) to offer you" has probably spent the better part of two days planning and preparing the meal. Of course, the guest should protest such disclaimers.

What is true of speaking about oneself or something one offers another person is also true of speaking about one's family. Because each person identifies so closely with one's family, to praise one's own spouse or children is a little like praising oneself. Japanese mothers, who are likely to be friends because their children are friends, will say how wonderful the other's son or daughter is, when in fact the mother's own son or daughter may be the brightest kid in the class. The reluctance to advertise the good qualities of one's immediate family is one reason Japanese find it strange when Western businesspeople keep pictures of their spouses or families on their desks at the office. "Is it because you miss your family so much that you keep their picture on your desk?" one Japanese asked an American. "No," said the American, "I guess it just helps to remind me why I'm here working." "Oh," said the Japanese, "then that's another difference between us." And yet, more than one North American intern in our research reported being surprised to hear some Japanese male friends in the office speak with great affection and appreciation of their wives and families. One intern said she was surprised because she had heard that men in Japan didn't compliment their wives; she said it gave her a new understanding of the kind of love and appreciation that men have for their wives and families which she thought she would never hear.

10. Face

Westerners who have had little contact with Asian cultures are likely to wonder about the concept of "face," which they have heard is extremely important. Is "face" comparable to what in some cultures is called "honor"? Or is it like what some people call "reputation" or "image"? Is the concern to save face and not to "lose face" a kind of cultural neurosis, an exaggerated worry about what others think, rather than something more tangible? When seen in the context of relationships, how one is regarded by others, and how one represents those for whom one is responsible is central. The difficulty that some people may have in understanding "face" in Japan stems largely from emphasis placed by Western values on the individual. The Japanese, in contrast, emphasize the group—the family, school, company—of which the individual is a part. From the Japanese perspective, therefore, how one treats others and is treated by them is of supreme importance, and so to slight another or to feel slighted, to cause embarrassment or be embarrassed, disturbs the delicate web of relationships that are essential to survival. What others think of a person really does matter in Japan.

The word "face" expresses very well this sense of how someone is seen or sees another. The Japanese mother teaches her child not to do or say certain things "or else people will laugh at you." This is a concern for face and appeals to the primary means of social control in the culture: shame. Japan is often identified as a "shame culture," where proper behavior is ensured through outside social pressure. This contrasts with the kind of controls identified with Western societies generally, where it is the internal feelings, like guilt, that are said to guide behavior. This is the matter of "conscience," or of being "God fearing." This well-known distinction between shame cultures and guilt cultures is, of course, not so clear-cut. Individuals everywhere can be very sensitive to what others say and think, and Japanese can be guided by an inner gyroscope that seems inalterable in the face of adversity. Nevertheless, concern for what others think, most importantly those others who constitute one's group, is a basic value and fact of life in Japan.

This sense of responsibility sometimes leads to taking one's life as a way of absolving others of responsibility. Suicide is an ultimate expression of taking responsibility. (Note that there are many reasons for suicide in Japan; taking responsibility in one's organization is only one.)

A person who is embarrassed in public—that is, in such a way that others become aware of it—shares that embarrassment with those of his or her group. A child who is disgraceful to her teacher brings shame on the child's family as well as on herself. A businessperson or government official who is embarrassed because he, or those for whom he is responsible, are shown to be incompetent or dishonest brings shame upon his group. That is why Japanese caught in such situations are much more likely to offer their resignations immediately rather than to fight things out. Taking full responsibility, particularly on the part of the person who is officially responsible, removes the burden that would otherwise have to be shared by others.

Shame is also used calculatingly to exert pressure. It sometimes happens that an employee in the United States who might be fired is, in Japan, simply given no more work to do. As a result, he or she may come to the office and have nothing to occupy the time at the office except reading the newspaper while colleagues continue to work away. Soon enough the feeling of shame will be such that the shunned has no face to show.

Seen in these ways, the concern with "face" is not exaggerated; it is an integral part of basic Japanese behavior aimed at managing interdependence and maintaining harmonious relations. There is not, therefore, the "preoccupation" with fears of losing face in Japan that some outsiders imagine, since it is usually in everybody's interest to maintain harmony. One is far more likely to lose face in Japan through making mistakes than from any intentional insult by others. Westerners who work closely with Japanese for some time will learn to be cautious in how they treat others, for fear of giving offense.

"Face" is also used in a positive sense in Japan. There is an expression that literally means a person "has a broad face," meaning the person is well known and has many, useful connections. Someone may even ask the one with the broad face, "May we borrow your face?" where elsewhere in the same situation someone might ask, "Can we use your name?" The slight difference in expressions is revealing: the "name" being what is given to the individual person, the "face" being that which is shown to others.

When Japanese work together with people new to the culture, problems related to "face" may arise. The most obvious, but not the most common, occurs when someone embarrasses a Japanese associate in public, either unintentionally or perhaps in the spirit of making a friendly joke without being aware of the discomfort caused or how detrimental it can be to future relations. (When face has been lost in Japan, it is much more difficult to reestablish good relations than is usually the case where identification with a group, family, or organization is not as strong.) An unintended slight is given most easily by younger or lower-ranking people who fail to express appropriate respect to an older or higher-ranking Japanese.

Japanese can be just as embarrassed when they are singled out for praise as for blame. Expatriate managers working in Japan can create problems when they single out, for example, one of several secretaries for praise. Although more subtle, it is an act of giving exceptional attention to one individual, of separating one from the group. Also, failure to include people who expect, as members of the organization, to be included can cause a loss of face.

However, it is also true that there are Japanese bosses who can be very direct in scolding an employee in front of others. Though less often seen in Japanese organizations today, this autocratic style within the group coexists with the concern for face

There is also much effort among Japanese to help "cover" for others, to work together to prevent or to "save" situations that might otherwise prove embarrassing to colleagues or friends. In this regard considerations of "face" may take precedence over other considerations, such as meeting a deadline, being consistent, or being frank about what is going on. One important means of avoiding loss of face for others is to pretend not to notice certain things that, if broached directly, could cause embarrassment. Even here, however, cultural differences may complicate the situation. A North American may want—or says he wants—frankly stated opinions of his actions. "I need your feedback," he may tell his coworker, "Please tell me if I offend you or do anything wrong so that I can learn and improve." But the Japanese are likely to be reluctant to give such opinions directly if they feel it would be embarrassing. It will serve one better to learn to read other signals, make one's own inferences, and test them out less directly in some appropriate setting with the right person. Conversely, the expatriate manager may have to temper "constructive criticism" or a "performance evaluation" so as not to cause unnecessary stress.

A Japanese executive who has worked almost equal amounts of time in Tokyo and in New York said he was amused by the American expression "to be thin-skinned," meaning "too sensitive to what others say." "I think Americans who work with Japanese need to become more thin-skinned, and Japanese who work with Americans—particularly in New York—need to become more 'thick-skinned,' because the meaning and consequences of what others say about us or how others treat us are so different in each country."

One other observation about "face." Two *kanji* (Chinese characters) are used for "face" in different situations. One is the word for face (*kao*), but another is the same as the character for "mask" (*mentsu/menmoku*), which may remind us that "face" is sometimes what we try to show outwardly (as when an English speaker might speak of "putting on a brave face") and not necessarily an expression of our true feelings. But as noted in the discussion of *honne* and *tatemae*, the outward expression can be just as valued as inner feelings.

For additional reading about the significance of "face" in intercultural communication, see Stella Ting-Toomey's, *The Challenge of Facework: Cross-cultural and Interpersonal Issues* (SUNY Press, 1994).

FIVE

In Place

Space and time are perceived as features of an objective reality. Space—and bounded places within—and time are also given shape by the cultures that we inhabit, and in anthropologist Hall's view these are at the heart of culture and the stresses that come with efforts to adjust to new cultural patterns. Our research found that for many of those from abroad who go to work in Japan, issues about "space" and "time" were *the* most often talked about. In this chapter and the following we discuss place and time in Japan.

THE CONTEXT OF PLACE: *BA*

Even as more and more communication occurs in cyberspace, in Japan, the physical context of communication, the places where people meet and talk, is integral and crucial. *Where* communication occurs is so important that it can easily determine *what* is likely to be said or shared and what probably will not. An employee may not want to complain directly to the boss at the office, but with a change of context, in place and time and often with the help of alcohol the employee can feel freer to open up—but one mustn't overdo it!—and the boss gets the message that might not otherwise be expressed. Indeed, the manager in this case may well have encouraged going out for drinks in the first place precisely to provide an appropriate place for other things to be said.

Much of the after-hours socializing by coworkers that Japan is so famous for takes place for the purpose of providing contexts for the kinds of interaction that do not occur during the workday but which are important for good interpersonal relations. Visitors to Tokyo, Osaka, or any large city in Japan are often surprised by the vast numbers of bars and small restaurants that fill the shopping and entertainment districts. In addition to providing what bars and restaurants do anywhere in the world, these also serve as the places where people from the office can go to talk about things and in ways that would not occur in the context of the workplace. Some serve as the settings for gatherings for officemates, *dōki*, and others, particularly at certain times of the year, such as December's *bōnen-kai* (a gathering to "forget the past year;" see Chapter 9).

UCHI AND *SOTO*

Two conceptual "places" that are far apart metaphorically but omnipresent in everyone's awareness are *uchi* (inside) and *soto* (outside). Japanese mark a clear distinction between what pertains to the family, school group, or company and matters that are outside of those domains. Thus, behavior that is considered appropriate within one's group may be quite different from the standards of behavior that is appropriate with people outside of one's group. This double standard is expected.

Professor Chie Nakane describes Japanese social relations as being divided roughly among three different domains: (1) within one's most intimate groups (uchi), beginning with the family but including other tightly knit in-groups; (2) in a social environment of engagement and collaboration; and (3) the outside (soto) world of the public—strangers. The polite behavior of bowing and apologies, indeed much of what is described in this book, is in that middle area—which has elements of both uchi and soto—with people with whom one socializes and works. Within the innermost group such politeness is not needed or, except on occasion, expected; nor does it apply in the outermost group, among the general public and strangers. So it is that the Japanese gentleman who in one situation seems exceedingly polite is later seen forcing his way into a crowded commuter train car.

Cultures differ about where and how one recognizes and maintains boundaries between what is my responsibility, what is none of my business, and that area in between. There has been a Japanese tradition of a homeowner's expected relationship with the homes on either side and the three directly across the street. These traditional norms break down in an urban landscape of high-rise apart- ments and condominiums. When a new person moves into a neighborhood— and even into an apartment building—there are ritual greetings with a token gift (traditionally soba, suggesting lines of connection), but in a more transient and mobile Japan, these are less often seen today.

So it is that coming to assist others with whom one has no formal relation- ship that falls into that middle area, and not just in Japan. When to get involved, when to stay out? What is valued assistance and what is intervention or med- dling?

When the Japan Overseas Cooperation Volunteer program was begun decades ago, the English word "volunteer" was used in the official title, as there seemed to be no equivalent in Japanese. One of its founders, Osamu Muro, said that because many Japanese did not understand the meaning of the organization's name, he would sometimes explain, "You know about the U.S. Peace Corps? Well, it's like that."

After the terrible Hanshin earthquake in Kobe in 1995, news reports gave considerable attention to the number of people from other parts of Japan who came to offer assistance in the aftermath. In an earlier time in Japanese history there would have been sympathy and concern, but unless one had relatives or close friends who suffered the devastation, there might have been fewer volunteers from across Japan who would have felt compelled to offer direct assistance.

Because the distinction between uchi and soto is important for any group, from large organizations to families, Japanese are very careful about whom they let in—that is, who is hired by the company, who is admitted to the university, and, of course, who is admitted into the family by marriage. Once admitted, however, the person becomes part of "us" and is not likely to be dismissed. Gen- erally speaking, few students in Japanese universities flunk out, though there are notable exceptions. The expectation for employees when hired is that, baring an economic situation that threatened the company, the employee will remain with the company until retirement.

Many of those who come to work in Japan do not make such a clear separa- tion, nor do they value the difficulty of entering and the expectation of remaining within groups and organizations. It is much easier for them to enter, leave, and move about from school to school, company to company, and from one marital relationship to another. This allows more freedom for the individual, which is so valued. This may also be part of a condition that many Western expatriates in Japan feel even after—or perhaps especially after—many years of living in Japan. It seems not unlike the experience of anyone who moves to a very traditional community anywhere in the world, where at first one is the newcomer, the outsider, and over time one is no longer that, and yet it may be generations before ever coming to feel like a complete insider.

FINDING ONE'S PLACE

Just as there is hierarchy in human relations that guide communication, there are also hierarchies in settings. In a traditional Japanese room, for example, there is a "low place" (*shimoza*) and a "high place" (*kamiza*), the former being a place to sit nearest the door, and the latter being away from the door with one's back to the *tokonoma* (where a flower arrangement or calligraphy hanging may be displayed). The person who serves tea or who goes in and out of the door to bring whatever is needed by the persons gathered at a meeting will sit in the "low place," nearest the door. The person who is the guest of honor, the eldest in the family, or the highest ranking person in the organization will sit in the high place. The only time there may be some appropriately performed dispute about who sits where is when a guest is politely declining the honor of sitting at the kamiza, an honor he or she will eventually accept.

Japanese books on etiquette and manners include guidance on seating arrangements for when a host or a guest is in the home, in a *washitsu* (tatami-mat room) in a Japanese restaurant, at the table in a Western restaurant, and even in a car. Circumstances, relationships, and a variety of practical considerations affect the seating arrangements in a car, but the formal place of deference is in the backseat behind the driver. For the visitor from abroad who is being treated as a guest, the best advice about seating is to slow down and let your hosts guide you so that they will not feel uncomfortable throughout the meeting or meal because you chose to sit in the wrong place.

THE OFFICE SPACE

The social amenities are important, but the space that seems to pose the greatest challenge to one who goes to work in Japan, especially during the first weeks or months, is the Japanese office. For someone who is accustomed to working in an office of cubicles, going to work in the open Japanese office can be daunting. The typical Japanese office layout is an open space with desks grouped together (*shima*, or islands) in rows, and the people work side-by-side, each facing someone on the other side of the shima.

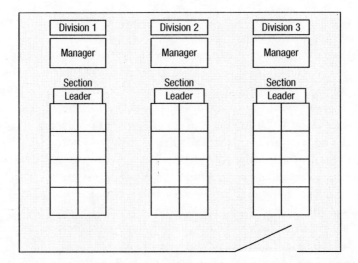

In Japanese offices it is much less common to see cubicles of the kind that first appeared in Western offices in the 1960s and which have become the norm in office environments and, as in the Dilbert cartoons, a central feature of office satires of "cubicle culture." North Americans who go to work for the first time in a Japanese office report feeling extremely uncomfortable, if not downright anxious to the point of paranoia. Exposed on their "island" in a sea of Japanese coworkers, aware of appearing different in physical appearance and behavior, unsure about what is expected, and often feeling insecure about their ability in speaking and understanding the Japanese language, the newly arrived expatriate in the Japanese office may look as uncomfortable as he or she feels. Not only is each person fully visible to others, every conversation, including phone conversations, can be heard by those who are seated nearby. And at the back of the room, overlooking the entire office, sits the manager.

Privacy is a concept that is not universal. The Japanese word for "privacy" is borrowed from the English. In parts of the West, privacy is a byproduct of individualism, and it is also associated with productivity—this being the rationale for the introduction of cubicles and private offices.

In the United States, people function well in their own private workspaces, such as cubicles separated by partitions. Generally, higher status means larger space and greater privacy. People also divide individual workspaces with a partition when a new person joins the group. For one accustomed to working on one project at a time, for the most part individually, distractions can mean disruptions in concentration and productivity. In contrast, when one has been accustomed to working as part of a group from the earliest years in school onward, privacy can feel more like isolation, separating oneself from the support one expects and can rely on. This extends beyond the immediate physical context of the office space; many Japanese who are transferred to a branch office overseas feel anxious about being out of the constant flow of information of all kinds, only some of which can be shared through the Internet or by phone.

Nearly everyone in our research who worked in Japanese offices and scientific and technical laboratories reported that their considerable stress in the first weeks at work eventually gave way to mere discomfort. Then, after a period of two to four months, the newcomers reported that they began to feel comfortable, and in time most said that they came to appreciate the open office setting for its many advantages. Some even said that when they came to the office each morning they felt like they were joining their team rather than "going to work."

While the disadvantages of an open work area were obvious to the interns from the beginning, the benefits of working in close proximity to others in a large open space slowly became apparent. "If I am having trouble with something, usually someone will notice and come to offer help—without my having to ask." When one wants to consult someone in the office about some project, he or she can usually see if the other person is on the phone, in a conversation, away from the desk, engrossed in work, or seems accessible. A large company's office space which could include even one hundred employees, may accommodate more than one division. In that case, communication across divisions can be facilitated by the open office arrangement.

All experts who were interviewed changed their attitudes about the physical space of their work environment after about six months or at the midpoint in their internships. From their initial feelings of anxiety because of the lack of privacy, they began to describe the setting in positive terms. After seven months into her job in Japan, one woman said:

When I worked in the U.S. I needed to make an appointment to see my boss. Here, my boss is sitting at a desk right across from mine. At first I felt like I was being watched all the time, but now I am getting used to it. I can see how he is doing this morning and he knows what I am doing for the day without saying a word. I like the fact that I am not isolated from everyone else. Whenever I look up from my computer I can see everyone in my section. I think that this leads to more interactions between coworkers. It is easier to exchange information. If I need help, I don't have to travel too far to get it. Right in front of you there is everybody. No cubicles, and all desks and everyone are in one big space. It took a lot of getting used to but I think after working in that environment I can work anywhere. But it was really difficult to get used to, a desk right here and a desk right there, people right next to you.

This reaction is representative of most of the others whose early anxiety about the open office space changed to positive feelings for the support the arrangement provided.

In a culture where the omnipresent nonverbal expressions can be more revealing than what is said, the open office is a principal medium of communication. We may exert most control over what we say, and least control in our nonverbal behavior—"more leakage," as the nonverbal expert Paul Ekman might say. As suggested in Chapter 3, in organizations and communities where meanings are principally invested in words, one is likely to ignore messages that are expressed nonverbally, such as movements, posture, and facial expressions. A U.S. manager of a Japanese company reported years ago that he was worried about having to report some bad news he had received from his headquarters to his office staff. He agonized for days about how to break the news, and then finally did so as best he could. Later he was told that everyone in the office had pretty much figured out the situation long before he told them. He later asked his secretary about that: "How did they know?" he wondered. She told him, "It was obvious from your face every time you came to the office."

SIX

About Time

In business and political worlds, people sometimes joke that a long-term plan in the United States is a short-term plan in Japan. In the U.S. "a long time" might be a year, or four quarters of a fiscal year. In Japan it is not uncommon for "a long time" to be at least thirty years, which until recently had been the normal cycle for an employee to work for a company. In a survey of thirty-one countries that take a long-term view in business, Japan ranked first, followed by Sweden; the United States ranked 19th. (See R.V. Levine, *A Geography of Time*, Basic Books, 1997.) This long-term view may characterize the overall outlook or managerial philosophy of an organization, and it also applies to more limited programs and projects within the company, including the hosting of Western expatriate workers, whose personal—even more than cultural—concerns with time follow a much shorter calendar. Some liken the difference to that between "marriage" and "dating."

A Japanese seasonal events calendar (see Chapter 9) shows twenty-four time markers, including the first day of spring and the dates of the solstice and equinox; several such seasonal markers are national holidays. The most important time-marker and holiday in Japan is the first day of the new year, for it marks the beginning of a new cycle, which is apparent socially and psychologically. During the final days of the year, one makes every effort to bring into balance both social and financial indebtedness. Not coincidentally, this is a time when bonuses are paid.

The business world also schedules events according to this seasonal calendar. New employees are hired each April, part of the rhythm of the year, with employees entering as a class, comparable to school matriculations. As noted earlier, this hiring system creates an invisible organizational stratification by age, with or without title, across divisions. Thus a person's age and seniority are closely related, making for greater predictability in maintaining harmonious interpersonal relations in an organization. It is into this pattern and rhythm that expatriates enter the organization, including interns, whose ages may be different from their Japanese counterparts, and whose point of entry is almost always "out of synch" with the rest of the newly hired.

TIME, ACTIVITY, AND RELATIONSHIPS

Not all cultures distinguish between "active" and "idle" time, but what constitutes each differs. The dominant value system in the United States has been characterized as a "doing orientation," and in much of the U.S. one's self-image is defined to a great extent by what he or she "does," with the most recent demonstrable individual achievements valued most. "Talk" in the U.S. has also been associated with "doing," so that in a meeting the absence of talk or the consciousness of silence is often experienced as "dead air," or a void needing to be filled. In contrast, the Japanese concept of *ma* is a meaningful pause, or a space that may contain deep feelings or a time to reflect on relationships, including power differences. It is a thoughtful pause, a time to process information, and a time to consider tactful responses. Thus silences within a meeting that Westerners may feel as awkward moments when "nothing is happening" are regarded in the context of a Japanese meeting as necessary and valuable.

Rikkyo University's Teruyuki Kume points out that Japanese prefer to use "group time" with the people with whom they are familiar, while Americans prefer to use "individual time" even within a group in order to expand their personal networks. Communication specialist Kume also notes the importance of the many ritual events in Japan, where people do things together without questioning—we do this because we have always done this, and we are missing something if we don't. Sharing group time with the same people creates a social tempo, a rhythm for the group. Thus in Japan, being present when people gather is often valued more than contributing individually at work.

For all these reasons, Japanese people do not so clearly separate work hours from after-work hours in the way that many Americans and other Westerners do. In Japan, one expects and values sharing time with other coworkers not just at work but afterwards, too. Overtime at the workplace is common, usually without expectation of additional compensation. In some cases a job simply requires overtime, but in other cases it is the value of the relationship with coworkers that requires "staying overtime." There is the sense of obligation, *giri*, that also explains the Japanese spending time with coworkers after work, which creates collective feelings of shared time together. It is not that Japanese employees are eager to spend extra hours with coworkers, but rather it is the recognition that this personal effort is appreciated as contributing to the group effort and morale, and as such is a valued personal quality.

TIME REQUIRED FOR ADAPTATION AND PRODUCTIVITY

Just how long does it take for an expat newcomer to become integrated into a Japanese organization? How long does it take to become an effective and contributing worker in an organization? Answers to these questions from the study's interviews showed some of the sharpest differences in expectations of interns and their supervisors.

When Japanese supervisors were asked how long it would take for an American intern to become integrated into the organization, they gave answers that ranged from "about one week" up to "a few months," depending, they said, upon the intern's personality. In interviews during the first six months, supervisors described their interns as generally getting along well. From the supervisor's point of view the crucial factor was that the interns had been introduced and approved by the appropriate administrators involving a government agency. As one put it, "They are part of our organization because they entered through the correct gate." This also means that a number of individuals and institutions outside of the host organization were regarded as part of the process and thus also partly responsible for whatever transpired during the intern's stay. (Permission to conduct this research similarly required the approval and support of these authorities.) In short, from the supervisors' point of view, newcomers by the very fact of their entry through the proper channels were part of the organization. The supervisors also made it clear in the early interviews that they cared about the interns and saw their relationship with the interns in terms of a teacher-student or as a parent-child relationship. Their time context was in terms of the intern's development rather than acceptance, which they took as a given.

From the interns' point of view, however, the immediate concern was with becoming accepted by their coworkers. When asked how long they thought this would take, the most optimistic interns said several months. Some said up to a year. Nearly half of the interns doubted that they would ever feel fully a part of a group. As reasons, they cited their status as an intern and the daunting challenge of the Japanese language. Even more than that, they felt that because of their appearance and that they were not Japanese, they would always be treated "as foreigners and as interns" (the two categories most often came together in the interns' comments).

Thus, while acceptance was a short-term concern from the supervisors' point of view, interns saw it as a long-term or even an insurmountable challenge. Comparing the comments of interns and their supervisors during the first six months, it was clear that they were operating on very different calendars: what the interns described and perceived as their uphill struggle for acceptance as they tried to adjust to their new situation, their supervisors saw as them already being accepted and well into their professional development.

When the question was asked about how long it would take for one to become an effective worker in the organization, however, the time estimates were reversed. The interns' estimate was minimal, but the supervisors' considerably longer, with an expectation gap of as much as five years.

The North American interns said it would take anywhere from a few weeks to a few months to get used to a job and to work as a productive member of the organization. Japanese supervisors, both those in engineering and in business, estimated between three and five years. According to the supervisors, even Japanese engineers require at least one year just to learn technical terms. Supervisors in research laboratories said that it would take a Japanese employee to be prepared as a research engineer from three to five years. One supervisor explained step by step why even a Japanese engineer would need as much as five years before being qualified:

> It will take one year to master the language, including technical words. In the second year, a new researcher will learn about the organization. In the third year, they will find out their role in the organization. Then they can start their own research and see results around the fifth year.

What seems striking, if not surprising, is the supervisor's emphasis on one's place within the organization, rather than emphasizing professional experience that leads to increased competence.

New researchers whose native language is not Japanese will need more time. Supervisors say that even for newly hired Japanese, it takes at least three years before they could effectively work as members of the organization. Managers see the first year as a training period, and that even a modest project would require at least two years to complete.

For those who do not have a technical background, the importance of language proficiency weighs even more heavily in job performance. A supervisor who had overseen an intern in his marketing section described the different expectations in language skills between interns in engineering and in business. Those who come to Japan with a background in science, technology, and engineering share a common language in their specialization and, to some extent, in their professional work routines.

In the business side, as in marketing or sales, the challenge of working in Japan is greater:

> If someone wants to be active in business, it is necessary to be fluent in the Japanese language. I don't even let new Japanese college graduates work with our clients. Those young Japanese who only use colloquialisms and abbreviations they hear on television programs have to spend four or five years to learn appropriate Japanese before they do business with our clients. Even if an overseas intern has an advanced degree, coming to our company is not the beginning of a career, but just the first step toward a career. For Japanese new employees, too, it will take at least five years.

In general, American interns perceive their job in terms of portable skills that they were responsible to learn individually, though with the help of others, and to apply wherever appropriate. They view effectiveness primarily in terms of task accomplishment, with the challenge of acceptance and adjustment as the principal barriers. Their Japanese supervisors see job effectiveness as contingent upon learning the context in which one will perform various tasks, and view one's job as part of a total package of professional abilities and interpersonal relationships that can be developed only over a period of time—all while learning how to play an effective role in the organization.

New expatriate workers saw developing good interpersonal relationships as getting to know other people and getting along with them. Many spoke in terms of friendships. For Japanese supervisors, however, the importance of interpersonal relationships means something different. It includes coming to understand which person is located in what part of the organizational network. When a newcomer wants to ask a question about the job, a general question about the company, seek advice for his or her career, or even ask for advice regarding one's personal life, the newcomer needs to know the right person to ask for each question. More than that, one also needs to know what other people might think if he or she chooses to ask person A rather than person B, or what meaning might be conveyed by failing to ask a particular person. For Japanese employees, this is one of the basic job skills they need to develop. It is something that cannot be learned in advance, and something that cannot be learned in a week or two. Japanese develop such consciousness and learn how to use their interpersonal antennae throughout their school days. It is so much a part of the culture that it may be difficult for those who are supervisors or coworkers to appreciate the difficulty of even being aware of this challenge that someone who is not from Japan faces, let alone the difficulty of developing the necessary sensitivity and skills.

This difference is consistent with descriptions of the respective cultural values, a more individualistic, "doing orientation" on the one hand, and a more relational orientation on the other. It would be an exaggeration to look only at these broad cultural differences. At the very least, however, these cultural differences may only amplify the different perspectives of a younger person in a transitory position working in another country and in a foreign language who is supervised by an older person with many years of working for an organization in a cultural environment in which he or she is most comfortable.

SHARED SPACE, SHARED TIME, AND SOCIALIZATION

By about the six-month period, most interns indicated a growing awareness of the importance of learning about, becoming more adept at, and feeling more comfortable in the interpersonal network of the organization. Their comments in interviews showed a noticeable shift from their concentration on defining their role and performing their assignments, whether in research or in the office, to socialization within the organization. Task was still important, but in their comments the process and the context of their work came to the fore. They arrived at this stage after struggling with two challenges regarding space and time: physical arrangement of the office or laboratory, and the time frame for working. As noted previously, during the first weeks and months of joining their host organization, all interns reported that the arrangement of the office and laboratory left them feeling exposed and vulnerable with no sense of privacy. The initial discomfort with the loss of privacy, over time, changed to an appreciation of the arrangement that requires constant involvement with others.

The orientation toward scheduled, organized time (monochronic time), the value of individualism, and a desire for privacy are all connected. When the clock shows that it is time to put away the day's work and leave the office or laboratory, to move from what one regards as work time and feel free to enter personal or private time, North Americans slowly realized that they might be the only ones clearing off their desks and heading for the door.

The following experience described by one intern is representative. She said that she still thinks about this long after completing her internship. Her assigned work hours were from 9:00 A.M. until 5:15 P.M. It was several weeks before she realized that nobody else left when she did at 5:15:

> I thought I was doing something wrong because everyone looked at me funny when I left. I didn't want to do anything wrong and I wanted to be more like the others in the group. I asked someone what I was doing wrong and why nobody else was leaving when I was leaving. They explained, "Well, it looks better if you stay until 6:00. Tomorrow, just stay until 6:00 and you'll notice that everybody leaves at 6:00." Actually, some of the women do leave right after 5:15 P.M., but [I later discovered] they were working in some other division. In my division people stay until 6:00. I felt bad because I thought the others thought I wasn't working as hard.

One person from Philadelphia, like most others reported about their early days of working in Japan, left the office as soon as he finished his work. Later he realized that other people stayed a little longer, although his section leader did not allow his staff to work overtime unnecessarily. He noticed that after the regular work hours the office atmosphere changed, people were more relaxed and talked about various things informally. In Japanese organizations this is a liminal time, no longer during regular office hours but not yet completely informal and personal. From then on he stayed later, sometimes working on his project and other times talking with others about job-related matters. Sometimes he just studied Japanese language at his desk. He discovered that during this period other people approached him, talked with him easily, and he soon came to know more about the group and began to feel a part of the group. What had initially seemed like a waste of time came to be appreciated as an essential part of his integration into the workforce. Near the end of his internship, his supervisor said in an interview that he had admired the intern's work ethic, including the fact that he talked little during regular work hours: "We [members of the division] often say that we chat too much. This smoothes our work flow [even though it takes us longer to complete some tasks]. To compensate, we stay a little longer than regular work hours." The supervisor also noted that his intern did not talk much when he was working, and the supervisor expressed appreciation for such professionalism, even though it was not the norm in the organization.

The supervisor's appreciation of the work habits of the man from Philadelphia who newly joined his group, and his appreciation of what goes on in a
Japanese office are revealing. He acknowledges that it is not unusual for people
in a Japanese office to work "after regular work hours," but says that it is because
the day-to-day social relationships that "smooth the work flow" are important.
He also admires the "efficiency" of the newcomer who concentrated on his task
and refrained from socializing. The Canadian may have taken refuge in work,
avoiding what may have been more challenging – to just chat with small talk
in a language he was still learning—but his efforts were appreciated. Yet the
supervisor notes that participating in the conversations that create the group
can't be lost for the sake of mere efficiency for a specific project.

Generally, throughout their time in Japan, it appears that those who first go
to work in Japan think of work hours as the time to complete their individual
tasks. For the Japanese coworkers, too, work hours are the time to do their jobs,
but they also see value in this as a shared time, starting at the same time, having
lunchtime together, and chatting and relaxing as they do their work. All this
strengthens interpersonal relations. It should also be noted that as the people
interviewed in our research adjusted to the physical and temporal constraints
and expectations of their workplace, their integration into the organization,
their personal comfort and satisfaction, and their competence in the Japanese
language all increased.

A SHORT-TERM VIEW, A LONG-TERM
VIEW, AND THE CONCEPT OF *EN*

The discussion in the previous section relates to a final theme about time that
in some ways runs through many of the issues explored here, a theme that also
may highlight some of the broader cultural distinctions regarding time: short-
term vision and long-term vision.

As noted earlier, the U.S. and Canadian interns and their Japanese supervisors held significantly different views on the time needed for one to become
an effective worker. These same views are also reflected in the observations by
supervisors about the interns' attitude toward jobs when the interns would ask if
the intern's work would be directly related to the development of new products.
One supervisor summarizes these differences clearly:

> He [the intern] wanted to know if the assignment would be used for
> a product. Our division is Research and Development. We do various

kinds of research. We don't know which results may be used for products. Some of the research we do is never used for a product. Other research work may be left for a few years and then it might be used to develop a product. We realize that such work is necessary, too. We need to spend time and energy to cover all kinds of research, often for small results. That's our job. The intern is very practical. He wants to know for what purpose he is doing the research. He wants to know how it will be used. He works hard with the research when he thinks the results will be used for sure, but he is not willing to do jobs that are not feasible to lead to products. [I can see that] the speed of his work and his effort on the job is different if it's a short-term project [with immediate application] or if it's a long-term project about which nobody knows if the research would be utilized in the future.

When the researcher later talked about this with the intern after he had returned to the United States, the intern expressed surprise. He said that from his limited work experience in the U.S. he thought that the Japanese supervisor's explanation would be unusual in the U.S. because of pressures to show a profit each quarter or at least by the end of each year.

The difference in time orientations appears more subtly in how work itself is regarded. While most interns were pleasantly surprised to discover that they could have their own research projects, many also remarked on how there was also "lots of time when I didn't have enough to do." From their supervisors' point of view, however, one's learning is never limited to one's own project. Rather, the supervisors value learning by observing, assisting senior workers over the years, and doing various menial jobs that might not seem directly relevant to their professional development. What the interns sometimes referred to as "idle time," the supervisors saw as opportunities for observation and learning.

This distinction in what is regarded as a productive time for learning has its counterpart in the interns' concerns about job differentiation, an issue apparent in comments of the North Americans and their supervisors, with some strong feelings expressed on both sides. From the interns' perspective, there are clear distinctions between "researcher," "assistant," and "administrator," and several interns balked at being asked to do jobs that they felt were "not part of the job description." In Japan, however, newly hired researchers assist senior researchers in order to learn the job. The U.S. interns expressed pride in being "researchers," and they resented being asked to do what appeared to be outside of that role. Their supervisors, in their comments in the interviews, indicated their irritation with that attitude and instead emphasized that from a long-term view of one's

71

development, even someone with a Ph.D. is not a competent researcher until he or she has learned about the whole organization, a process requiring many years of assisting and observing.

It was mentioned earlier that supervisors welcomed the interns but without expectations of any production benefit from their contributions, because from their perspective, even a two-year stay would be too short. But several supervisors spoke of the possibility of benefits far in the future that could not be clearly anticipated right away. They often spoke of *en*, which means a kind of "connection by destiny," or as communication scholar Satoshi Ishii explains, a relationship beyond any rational explanation. Professor Ishii has helped expand notions of communication through Buddhist and other non-Western perspectives, including very different ideas of time and human relationships. Whatever might happen in the future regarding these interns and their former supervisors or coworkers would be because of *en*, something "that was meant to be," though just *what* could not be anticipated. Thus while those who came to work in Japan may want to evaluate their experience at the end of several months or years, their supervisors are imagining effects that may not be recognized for perhaps twenty years or more. Japanese supervisors did not talk to the interns about their long-term view, though even if they did it might not have altered the interns' focus on much more than the immediate and demonstrable results.

In summary, as Patricia Gercik, the veteran director of the pioneering M.I.T. Japan Program, says, it is in the day-to-day experience of working in Japan that an individual from one culture must negotiate adjustments to work in the other. It is not so much a matter of "knowing about Japan" in general terms. Where individual effectiveness is the focus, the "results" or "goal orientation" is emphasized, while those from the West often do not fully appreciate that the long-term "process orientation" is fundamental to those working in a Japanese organization.

It appears that it requires about four months for those going from North America to adjust to the Japanese use of office space, which offers much less privacy. In this time the interns came to appreciate the social support and opportunity to integrate further into their group that resulted from time shared with others, even after their official workday was over. After around six months, interns spoke less about wanting more private or personal time. However, there were other issues they could not figure out until the end of a year of working in Japan, if then. One of the most important was the issue of gaining feedback on their work, a subject not unrelated to time and space considerations. We discuss this in the next chapter.

SEVEN

Waiting for Feedback

"I worked on projects in the lab for more than a year in Japan before I returned to the U.S. I have no idea what my supervisor thought of my work, whether I was successful or not. I never received any feedback." This remark, reflecting puzzlement and disappointment, has been echoed by many people from North America, Europe, and elsewhere when they go to work in Japan—by nearly 80 percent of those interviewed in our research and by other observers as well. But one Japanese supervisor explained this from a different point of view. "For us, we don't think feedback is necessary. I think it's a cultural difference. In Japan, if we don't have any complaint or any particular comment, that means the best evaluation. But it seems that for people from the U.S., if there is no comment, they think there is a problem."

Of all the differences in expectations, perceptions, and behavior that characterize intercultural communication when people from abroad work in Japanese organizations, the issue of "feedback" ranks near the top of the list. The Japanese language borrowed the word "feedback" from English (as they did the word "communication"). It is pronounced "feed-o-bock-ku" (*fīdobakku*), and such terms are written in the Japanese phonetic syllabary, *katakana*, which is used to indicate words borrowed from a foreign language. As in English-language dictionaries, most Japanese dictionaries cite the source of the original definitions, and fidobakku is listed as being from electronics and biology. For fidobakku, other meanings include a reaction (to a talk), a suggestion, and a response (from the audience, readers, etc.). The respected Japanese dictionary *Kōjien* defines fidobakku as relating the information regarding the results of one action to the next action. In some Japanese dictionaries, fidobakku is also defined as "evaluation" (*hyōka*), although hyōka suggests a more formal evaluation than does fidobakku. From its source in electrical engineering or biology, many Japanese consider feedback as a process to modify behavior based on the information received from the results, but not all Japanese think of feedback as a process of modification or improvement in human communication or in the learning process. Moreover, within a Japanese organization, the concept of feedback is not nearly as widely used nor does it have the same connotation as for Western organizations. In short, across cultures the origins of the concept of feedback are the same, but its applications are different.

In the West, feedback is typically categorized into two types: positive and negative. The response to negative feedback is to change behavior, such as reducing or ceasing something altogether. Positive feedback, on the other hand, encourages the behavior—to continue or perhaps to increase doing what one is doing. Americans are encouraged to motivate their children through positive feedback, praise. Their preferred model of childrearing is acknowledging positive behavior and rewarding it. However, as noted previously, the Japanese rear their children differently. For example, the coauthor of this book was rarely praised by parents for achievements at school. Rather, the encouragement was to do better; a score of 98 percent on a test might be met with a question about that other 2 percent.

The style of feedback in childhood leads to the preferred style of feedback in the workplace. American managers compliment workers who have done a good job, and consider praising the individual important in motivating Americans in the workplace.

Japanese (and Asians generally) also may praise someone in public, but for different reasons and much less frequently than the typical American manager. Japanese give public praise to promote face, while Americans praise to motivate performance. Also, the kind of words used for praising may differ across cultures. Superlatives—"wonderful," "great job," "terrific accomplishment!"—expressed frequently can ring hollow to Asian ears.

In different cultural contexts feedback is used in other ways, and its expression or absence, rooted in a lifetime of experience, is interpreted and felt differently. Employees may lose motivation or be unable to improve their performance without the desired form of feedback. In another context, giving effusive feedback to motivate employees may cause a loss of face in front of coworkers, and even loss of trust of the manager if he or she too often expresses what seem like excessive praise for routine work.

When asked about feedback given while working in Japan, more than 90 percent of the interns responded that they did not receive enough—or any—feedback from their Japanese supervisors. These are some representative responses to the question, "Did you receive feedback from your supervisor?"

> I asked three Japanese supervisors questions about how I was doing but [I was given] no feedback. They talked about a "progress report" but [gave] no specific feedback.

> [My instructor] and I were the only two working on [my assigned project]. He had many other things to do. Most of the feedback I would get was, "Whatever you want to do, just get it done." Well, okay, but I really wanted to have more feedback.

> I didn't get enough evaluation. If something was really good, they didn't say too much. They'd just say, "This was good." That's it. If there was a problem, they were very subtle, "Maybe we need to fix this area." I guess they kind of expected me to be good anyway, so they shouldn't have to praise me. Americans expect more feedback, "This is good, could be better, we expected more, etc." I just don't hear enough of that. In the end I heard that they were very glad about my working there. But you never know if that was just a nice thing to say because you were leaving.

> I would have liked to have a little bit more of, "This is what you're doing well" and "This is what you could improve on," and get some feedback so that I knew where some of my weaknesses were and knew what my strengths were as well [and] ideas on how to improve them. I think that's a very important process when you're reviewing people. I know when I review my people, I try to do that—tell them what they're doing right, what I think they're not doing right, and then how they can improve on what they're doing right and what they're not doing right. There's always room for improvement, right?

With feedback especially, fluency in the Japanese language and picking up on subtleties is important, but even those with the highest levels of spoken Japanese expressed frustration at not receiving sufficient feedback. One intern whose Japanese language ability was strong made this observation:

> I have not received any feedback on any of my work, except for corrections to my weekly reports, which are written in Japanese. When I am assigned

a task, I pursue it to the best of my ability. But when I don't have a clearly defined task, I am at a loss as to what I should be doing.

Although most of those who spoke about their work in Japan said that they did not receive the feedback they expected, several said that they were given some kind of feedback. One who said that from his intercultural training before going to Japan he was prepared to receive no negative comments, and so was surprised at how his supervisors gave him feedback, and though the style differed from what he was used to, he said he came to appreciate the learning style he experienced with his supervisors. But these were exceptions, and are more likely to be offered by supervisors who have been advised that North American interns need more encouragement.

The same pattern has been reported in studies of Japanese subsidiaries in the United States, with Japanese supervisors and U.S. workers. Prof. Hiroko Nishida, who has studied Japanese subsidiaries abroad, quoted American workers who complained that Japanese do not explain what they expect of their employees. The Americans express frustration when they do not receive any feedback after they complete their jobs, especially when they feel that they have done a good job and expect to hear some words of praise.

JAPANESE SUPERVISORS' PERCEPTIONS OF GIVING FEEDBACK

Are Japanese supervisors aware that they don't provide the feedback that the North Americans expect? As noted, fīdobakku is commonly used in Japanese organizations without a consistent or clear definition, and can include the meaning of hyōka (evaluation). Supervisors who were asked if they gave feedback or evaluations reflected on what they did and didn't do, and then responded that they often meet with and check with workers they are responsible for. When pressed to say if they give specific feedback, the supervisors said that they usually do not do so explicitly. There is no expected form, no model; rather, it depends on interpersonal relationships and context. From the supervisors' point of view, feedback is more about listening and sensing someone's progress and then giving instructions rather than evaluating the person's work.

In addition to the general differences in ideas about feedback in Japan and for many who come from abroad to work in Japan, there are notable differences in expectations across cultures about how, what, where, and when feedback will be expressed.

EXPLICIT AND IMPLICIT
COMMUNICATION

From childhood, North Americans mostly expect that feedback will be clear, explicit, and expressed verbally. The interns indicated that they expected all kinds of feedback, including constructive criticism, so that they could learn and improve. As seen in the comments by supervisors, Japanese may feel that they are always giving a kind of "feedback" through their behavior, though not necessarily verbalized. Consultants Clifford Clark and Douglas Lipp pointed out that different expectations toward positive and negative feedback cause frustration for both Japanese managers and American subordinates, and because the different expectations arise from how one was reared, expecting "positive feedback" for some and a reluctance to give such praise for others is not limited to superior-subordinate relationships in an organization. (See Clifford Clarke and G.D. Lipp, *Danger and Opportunity: Resolving Conflict in U.S.-Based Japanese Subsidiaries* (Intercultural Press, 1998).

Japanese "how-to" guidelines that have been published for Japanese managers working with North American subordinates encourage managers to "praise your subordinate with exaggerated expressions even if you feel embarrassed." In Japan the usual form of praise, however, is more subtle. One often sees a scene in movies or in television dramas in which a manager just quietly reads through a proposal that a subordinate took months to prepare and then says, "Okay" without looking up. This kind of reaction may be hard to understand for people who are not accustomed to it, but if one knows the supervisor or manager well, and if that is his or her style, it is not only acceptable but also considered as positive feedback in that context. This may be related to the previously noted cultural history of distrust of words.

Even among the majority of expat workers in Japan who indicated that they did not receive feedback, they noted that the advantage of their close proximity to coworkers and their supervisor made it easy to receive reactions from others about their work, even if this was not precisely the kind of explicit feedback that they expected or wished for.

POSITIVE AND NEGATIVE FEEDBACK

Although the interns mentioned that they wished to have any kind of feedback, the lack of positive feedback in particular made them anxious, in part because for many it was their first work experience abroad, and for all because even if they had years of experience, this was their first time working in Japan. They wanted to learn from their experience, and hoped to receive confirmation that they had done well. As noted, Americans seek and anticipate direct and almost immediate verbal confirmation that they are doing well. From a Japanese perspective, the new Western workers seem to expect to receive explicit positive feedback when none is called for, since everything is all right—no news is good news—while from the Westerners' perspective, the absence of positive feedback is frustrating and lessens their confidence in their work.

North Americans working in Japan may hope to receive critical feedback, or at least constructive criticism, in the form of suggestions for improvement. Previous studies report not only that Japanese managers give little or no positive feedback, but also indicate that Japanese managers are viewed as giving too much critical feedback and not enough positive feedback. As noted in the discussion of "face," in some traditional Japanese organizations it is not surprising to witness supervisors scold subordinates in front of others. This kind of behavior may seem to make subordinates lose face and therefore seem to contradict Japanese sensitivity to issues of face, one's own and that of others. One interpretation of this form of negative feedback in the form of scolding, rather than more conventional "constructive criticism" might be considered. This is what happens within the family (uchi), the irritated patriarch's scolding of his children. This open outburst of "feedback" is much less likely to be experienced directly by the Western expatriate in part because he or she might never been regarded (at least by the imagined martinet scold) as fully inside the group. Another interpretation of such public (in the office) scolds, mentioned by several supervisors is that if a manager picks on one person in a group, that person will gain sympathy from the others. In that way the manager plays the role of the "bad guy" so that the rest of the group will further bond together as a team.

TIMING AND LOCATION OF FEEDBACK

When and where one expects feedback also differs across the cultures. Some interns expressed their frustration about not receiving any comments after their presentations or even when they finished their internships and were about to return home. The interns wanted to know, "How did I do?" The Japanese supervisor may take a broader perspective, looking at the whole project, with the input of many workers involved, and viewed in the long term. In the interviews the supervisors said that they could have given some comments on what the interns contributed, but they would rather wait until the results of the entire projects were clear.

The timing of feedback may be crucial, for if there is a time lag between performance and feedback, those expecting immediate feedback may feel there is no feedback. People say that they want to hear as soon as it seems feasible and appropriate, not weeks or months later. Delayed feedback will frustrate and cause one to sigh, "*Now* you tell me!" Differences in expectations regarding timing also contribute to a perception of Japanese supervisors being vague in offering feedback. Even explicit feedback might not be recognized as such if it is given during a morning's debriefing, a meeting for checking the schedule and progress of an internship, or a reflective meeting for a project with other team members. Some supervisors commented they gave feedback every morning when they met their interns, while others said that they gave feedback when they went out with those they supervised for a meal or after work for drinks. Different meanings of time and place are a part of the different perceptions of feedback.

One intern who remarked that she had learned "the Japanese style of communication" said that she could receive more feedback when she went out for drinks with her supervisors than she received at work. She said that in the United States she would hesitate to go out with her supervisors after work, but in Japan she realized that going out for a drink was not so much a personal matter as it was a continuation of her work. Most importantly, it provided a time and place where she could ask questions and seek advice freely.

In this case the feedback was explicit and sometimes even negative, but the intern was able to improve her performance based on the comments. However, as the intern observed, it took her a few months to learn when and where she could expect to receive the feedback she was seeking.

VISITING RESEARCHERS

For expatriate researchers in Japan who work on projects that last for months or longer, expectations for feedback are understandably especially high. Most of the interns in our study who worked in Japanese labs reported that they received little or no such feedback. A supervisor who required her interns to present one-month progress reports asked questions during the presentations, and the person assigned as the intern's instructor then gave the next project for the intern to work on. The supervisor said that she did not mention any particular kind of feedback, but that she considered the questions asked during the presentations and the topics the interns were assigned for the next project the appropriate form of feedback. While the interns anticipated some verbal feedback at the time of their presentation, their supervisors considered that the presentation itself was a kind of evaluation and therefore did not merit any further comment. They assumed that the occasion to present his or her results was itself an affirmation of the intern's achievement. Supervisors say that because of the nature of research projects, they could not be sure of the results of any project immediately and therefore usually cannot give an evaluation of someone's work even if he or she is about to leave Japan and return home.

GENDER CONSIDERATIONS

Although the number of data is small, there is an indication of a difference between the perceptions of feedback related to gender. Some may see this as reflecting the widely supported view that women pick up on nonverbal communication more than men and are more sensitive to nuance. Some may be suspicious that male supervisors will be more generous with Western female subordinates in explaining what they assume is not needed for their male counterparts. There are other interpretations, and in any case the data are limited, but most of the females interviewed reported that they did receive feedback, though many said that there was not enough "verbal feedback." One woman was at first dubious about meeting after hours with her male supervisor until she realized that others did as well. She reported that these times were when she received the most meaningful and honest feedback on her performance and when she could freely ask any questions regarding her job and her future career. These after-hours meetings allowed for a much broader discussion about career and life goals that would not have been possible at work.

Expecting to learn how one is doing and how to improve through explicit verbal feedback may not be the best way to learn on the job in Japan. Sometimes this may be due to the curiosity and uniqueness of connecting across the cultures, or it may be due to the ability or personality of the manager, supervisor, or mentor. It may also arise from different expectations of how best to learn and to foster that learning. For someone who is going to work in Japan, it may require a broader view of ways of learning, the subject of the following chapter.

EIGHT

八

On-the-Job Learning

To learn, and to continuously learn: this is one of the most important values in Japan, traditionally and today, and is recognized and admired far from its shores. In business, industry, and technology, the Japanese word *kaizen* (improvement) has become internationally identified with a philosophy of continuous improvement, where one believes there is always room for improvement. We see that in a parent's reluctance to praise a child for work well done so that the child will be encouraged to strive to do even better.

THE MANY WAYS OF LEARNING

As in much of the world, the teacher is esteemed and honored long after his or her students have gone their separate ways. In the traditional arts of *kadō* or *ikebana* (flower arrangement), *chadō* (tea ceremony), *shodō* (calligraphy), and the martial arts, the master holds a place of significance, and teachers in Japan today are highly respected; their value cannot be measured by their income. It is notable that one of Japan's most famous cultural exports is the teaching of those traditional arts. But though the model of "the way," and the wisdom of what the *sensei*, if not master, offers, this tradition of learning is rarely the way those who go to work in Japan will learn on the job. There are other fundamental ways, equally grounded in Japan but less famous or formalized.

In this chapter we look at ways of learning on the job—and after work hours, too—with insights from the anthropologist Edward T. Hall. Hall introduced the idea that not just what we learn, but how we expect to learn, is a deeply rooted part of our cultural upbringing and therefore also a part of what happens when we go to work in a new environment. Going to work in Japan is a new experience for most readers of this book, but attention to how one is accustomed to learning and expects to be taught or coached or mentored (each word suggesting a different idea of learning) is a part of everyone's life and irrespective of travel overseas. Of the many insights, and concepts that Hall introduced, the area that he thought might be the most important is one that has received relatively little attention: ways of learning. In Japan it is an area that reveals much about the culture and about intercultural relations for those going to Japan. Hall distinguished among three kinds of learning: formal, technical, and informal. In Japan each of these plays an important role at the office and laboratory—no less than in the classroom.

FORMAL LEARNING

Formal learning involves a teacher and student. The teacher may be a supervisor or a more experienced coworker. (At home, the teacher is most often a parent or older brother or sister. At work the formal teacher would be the one assigned to advise and assist, and to train. The teacher, master, or supervisor shows "the way." As mentioned earlier, the "-*dō*" in *shodō*, *judō*, and other traditional Japanese art forms, tranquil or martial, means "the way," or the path. In Japan there is often a right way, or best way, of doing something and many wrong ways. As Hall pointed out, doing something the wrong way will provoke an emotional response: "*No!* Not *that* way!" The way to learn the way is to learn the pattern or form and repeat, repeat, repeat. Observation is more important than paying attention to words spoken.

When one is first learning in a formal relationship, it is appropriate—even expected—that the one learning will ask questions about something not well understood. (One should not ask the same question too many times, however.) In Japanese companies, an employee's first year is the time when questions should be asked. Some interns from the United States reported that they were nervous about asking questions for fear of seeming less competent than they wanted to appear. This was especially true for those who joined a company for a period of more than a few months and who presented themselves as professionals, not interns in a learner role. This was also true generally of those who were in their late twenties or older and who had come with experience that they believed they would be contributing to their organization. In contrast, those who were younger, less experienced, and who saw their role as learners seemed less guarded about expressing their unfamiliarity with a process. They were not uncomfortable about asking questions. Canadian interns who came as part of their co-op program while still undergraduate students—who were younger, whose role in Japan was not so different from work roles in the Canadian co-op program felt less vulnerable and were more comfortable about asking questions. Those who felt they had more on the line, more to prove, were also were more reluctant to ask questions and to feel anxious about asking questions.

Formal learning works when the relationship of teacher and student is clear. As one goes across cultures, recognizing this relationship can be problematic when by circumstance one must be a student but does not want to appear to be a beginner. At a language class this may be no problem; at work, the ambiguity or feeling a need to prove oneself can be a problem.

TECHNICAL LEARNING

Technical learning is also directed toward a correct or best way to do something, but in a form that does not require the presence of a real-life teacher. For example, technical writers convert what has been covered in formal or informal (described in the next section) learning into dispassionate and "user-friendly" forms in printed or online documentation that all users can access. The voice that models a foreign language one is studying is one example of "technical" learning. Increasingly, one learns through this dispassionate, disembodied teaching form. The "technical" impact on other ways of learning is a major social phenomenon of our time, in Japan no less than elsewhere. In Japan, as everywhere else, many things that previously would have been taught personally are now taught in this mode, sometimes because the traditional teachers are no longer available to everyone. Juzo Itami's classic film *Osō-shiki* (*The Funeral*) was inspired by the late director Itami's experience of needing to perform his role in a family funeral and, with no family member to advise him, he had to rent a video to learn how to act.

INFORMAL LEARNING

In adapting to work in another culture, informal learning is the most important of all. "Informal learning" may be a misleading term, for this is not the same as casually doing what one wants to do or improvising when one doesn't know what to do. Rather it is how one learns through observation and trial and error. Often it is a kind of learning that happens when one is less conscious of learning than when one assumes the role of learner. It is the way we as children became enculturated; it is the way we learn our mother tongue, so different from how we learn another language in a formal classroom. Linguists use the term "language acquisition" for how we come to speak our first language to distinguish it from "language learning," which requires our conscious attention to models and rules.

Observation is key. Highly valued is the one who catches on quickly: *"Sasshi ga hayai"* is a high compliment in Japan. This quality is important for the formal learner, too, of course, but especially for the person who catches on without having to be told in so many words. Perhaps the most famous model of this kind of informal learning in Japan is that of the person who wants to learn to become a *rakugo-ka*, a traditional storyteller entertainer. In the folklore version, at least, the apprentice goes to work for the rakugo-ka master, doing all manner of menial work—cleaning the house, shopping, whatever is required. This goes on for a very long time, and without any explicit instruction by the master on how to become a rakugo-ka. And then one day, the master tells the apprentice, "Now you are ready."

Apprenticeship held a significant place in learning in Japan until about sixty years ago, but some of the features of that style of informal learning remain. The contract that a new employee receives often presents only the most general job descriptions; what one will be expected to learn and do will be gained through the experience of being on the job. The first year on the job may consist largely of seemingly menial tasks—unpacking and shelving materials, sorting mail, and the like. But in the process one is expected to informally learn a great deal about the organizational structure and interpersonal relations within the organization. "Time" is not a teacher, but time is essential for this kind of learning—no formal or technical means can fully replace all that to which one is apprenticed.

One of the interns interviewed in our study expressed his experience of learning on the job this way:

> I think most people go into [their internship] most worried about a language barrier and then realize that the language barrier is the least of the

challenges. More than that, though, I would say that the thought process is different for the Japanese employee and for an American employee. So you need to learn how to think the same way that they do. For example, the way that the Japanese supervisors teach . . . there's a lot of showing by example, and they expect you to pick up on what they show you—how you deal with people, the types of situations when you speak, the types of situations when you allow the customer to speak, things like that. I sensed that for a lot of the interns from the States, if they don't have a direct explanation, they don't usually pick up on it.

This observation may be an important part of the differences regarding feedback discussed in the previous chapter. Japanese supervisors thought they were doing all that was needed for the interns, while most of the workers from the United States were waiting for formal, explicit comments.

For someone from outside of Japan who joins a Japanese organization as an intern or as a contract employee, and even for an exchange student who will study at a Japanese university for a year, the Japanese value of apprenticeship learning poses some obvious challenges. What can one learn in only six months or a year? What expectations should the host organization have for someone who has come for a relatively short time and with a limited commitment to the organization? Some professional people are hired with the expectation that they will be able to be effective immediately. In today's economic situation, detailed manuals may be given to new hires so they can do certain kinds of work right away. However, informal learning is still valued as a means for an employee to become fully capable in the organization.

TIME AND PLACE AND INFORMAL LEARNING

As noted in Chapter 6, an experience that nearly all the interns in our study reported was discovering that their workday did not end at 5:00. Rather, the norm was to remain in the office for some time into the evening. Many of the interns said that after first trying to figure out what to do and grumbling that it was a waste of their personal time, that it was in the evening at the office when they came to feel more comfortable and began to learn about others and the organization in ways that did not occur during the formal workday. This became a time for informal learning that proved to be the most valuable of all.

The newcomer to Japan may be overly influenced by the boundaries of formal times and places (9:00 to 5:00 at the office or lab) and not see opportunities that are considered most important for many Japanese in the same situation. In the classroom, the preferred times for interactions between students and their teachers are often right before and especially right after the class, rather than during the flow of the formal classroom or even in the instructor's office. In organizations, what takes place during the formal meeting is often more a ratification or public enactment of decisions already reached through longer, more varied, and often informal engagements of those involved.

What is said after hours in a relaxed setting or expressed nonverbally is often crucial but less likely to be expressed at other times and in other formal settings.

ASKING QUESTIONS

Those who go to work in Japan often have questions about asking questions. As discussed earlier, our interviews revealed that many of the interns from the United States were reluctant to ask questions about their assignments in the office or in the laboratory, mostly because they feared that this would raise doubts about their competence. This seemed less an issue for women than for men. It was rarely mentioned by the Canadian interns whose presence was more clearly in the role of learner (they hadn't graduated from college yet) than for many from the U.S. who were older, some with graduate degrees, and most with more professional experience. So one question about asking questions is why one might be nervous about this—for reasons arising from the Japanese work culture or for reasons more related to one's own feelings of being in a new setting and understandably concerned how he or she will be judged by others.

In Japanese organizations, asking questions about work, especially during the first year, is expected and encouraged. This is a crucial time for learning about the organization and how things work. For Westerners who go to work in Japan only for a year or two, however, "the first year" may be their entire time, so some of the reluctance is understandable. Japanese supervisors interviewed did not seem particularly concerned about questions being asked, and when the issue was raised they seemed surprised to hear about the reluctance.

Asking questions is part of formal learning; learning through not asking questions is part of the important informal learning. Anthropologist Hall advised his graduate students venturing into a new setting to do their ethnographic field work to not ask questions. His reasons apply to those who go to work in Japan, which might be likened to one doing ethnographic work: try to figure out how things work by watching because often no one can answer that question since they are so much a part of the process. It can also result in a kind of awkwardness that parents sometimes feel when their children ask some very good questions that are not easy to answer simply.

There is another reason for not asking certain kinds of questions. Professor Kichiro Hayashi advises those going to work in Japan not to ask questions, because in Japan it may be more important to pay attention to much that cannot be put in words—to be able to sense the mood (*kūki*), notice the posture and demeanor of others, and get some idea of what is going on, to continually test, affirm, or revise one's impression. It exercises one's ability to work within a degree of ambiguity, which is almost always the case in working in a cultural setting where one is always learning.

LEARNING AWAY FROM THE JOB

The interest in going to work in Japan arises, for so many people, from an earlier curiosity and serious interest in things Japanese that seem to have almost nothing to do with one's professional work. Many of those who want to live and work in Japan became curious about Japan when they first saw Japanese animation cartoons or films (*anime*), comics (*manga*), or joined a martial arts class. It works the other way, too, of course, with Japanese who love the music, films, and sports that come from overseas but are so familiar in Japan. Japanese popular culture and export versions of traditional Japanese arts sparked an interest that led to working in an office, schoolroom, or laboratory. These initial interests stimulate a different part of the brain from that which is stimulated in the work setting, and they reward once more the expatriate working in Japan. Those whose work experience in Japan seems most satisfying and enduring are those involved in other aspects of the culture outside of the workplace. It seems not to matter what the interest is, or even if it is totally separate from work. Those who seem most happy at work are the same people who pursue the interests that first led them to make a connection with Japan, or who found something that engaged them after arriving. For many it was physical—sports, kendo, or other Japanese martial arts, or Western sports, such as pick-up basketball games or something more fundamental such as running. For others it was less physical—music (surprising how many people found their way into Japanese musical groups), or photography or contemporary popular art. (Even low rider cars, a fine contemporary Chicano folk art, has a presence in Japan—indeed, Japan may now host the world's best lowrider cars and publications—and the same is true of so many interests that one might have thought were exclusive to other regions.) Sometimes one's personal interests and aptitudes happen to fit what a host company likes. A major manufacturing company benefited from the talents of a woman from Canada who became a star on their otherwise all-male baseball team.

Away from the job one is almost certain to learn informally, to learn without the emotional pressures and self-consciousness that are a part of working as a professional in the organization. The friendships formed will be different, the occasions of getting together will also be different; the competence and confidence in using the Japanese language, and even the kinds of questions asked and exchanged, will almost certainly be different and more personal, which can also offer the most valuable and memorable learning about the host culture.

NINE

九

In Sync with the
Rhythms of the Year

We are all influenced by the rhythms of work and the different rhythms of play, of conversations, and the ambient sounds that are a part of the culture, as well as by the rhythms of a day, a week, a month, a season, a year, and the cycle of years. In its agricultural history (until the 1950s, more Japanese lived on farms than in cities), and its animistic *Shintō* influences that are never far from the surface, its aesthetic sensitivities and expressions, and even in the workplace, people in Japan pay close attention to the seasons. Anyone who goes to work in Japan must also pay attention, for this is the heartbeat of the culture. At root may be the desire to be in harmony with nature, which in turn relates to being in harmony with others at work, where there are busy times and slow times, the season to welcome and the season to say farewell.

Anticipating the events that mark or influence the rhythms of the national culture and the various organizational cultures can help someone new to working in Japan feel more in sync with others at work and with the society as a whole. The days around the New Year holiday in January are very different in Japan than the celebrations in much of the West, even if the dates coincide. In Japan it is a pause, a quiet time, a time for family and renewal of friendships. Then there is another beginning in April when the new recruits enter their companies and when the new school year begins. These and other events, some formally recognized, set the pace and the tone for the year. In this chapter we include some of the most important days and seasons of the year that affect many aspects of communication and conventions at work and in daily life. For more detailed information, there are many fine books on holidays and events and their histories that one can purchase. In this chapter we hope to give the reader a feel for the rhythm of the year and an appreciation of the opportunity to feel more in sync with the nation.

Japanese work culture pays attention to the beginning and ending of the year. There is the day that marks the first workday of the new year (*shigoto-hajime*) and a day that marks the last workday of the year (*shigoto-osame*). The former often means special attention to dress and may include speeches by company officers; the latter may mean employees working to clean up the office, laboratory, or other workplace before leaving for the New Year's break. The Japanese New Year follows the nearly world-standard Gregorian calendar, with the first day of January as the first day of the new year; it is also emotionally and symbolically the most important date on the calendar. But the Japanese new work year actually begins in April, as does the new school year. As mentioned earlier, newly hired employees begin in April, so the experience of someone who goes to Japan to work starting in April will be very different from the experience of one who arrives in, say, August—typically one of the slowest work times and a month marked by *Obon*, when many people travel to their ancestral home, and may also enjoy a brief but well-earned vacation.

No two companies are alike in their organizational culture or particular rhythm, so it is important to try to gain a sense of the flow and pace that characterizes the days, weeks, and seasons of the organization into which one has entered. Generally, however, and at a national level, two of the busiest times are in the months just before the new formal beginnings. December is busy with finishing up personal, social, and work-related obligations before the end of the calendar year; it is also a time of *bōnen-kai* (end of the year) parties, and the season of shopping for commercialized Western holidays that has overtaken Japan as well. It is also the month when a bonus may be paid. March may also be busy in anticipation of the new work and new academic year that begins in April, and thus there will be a flurry of meetings as well as planning training and social activities to integrate those new to the organization.

In every society the seasons and special days are associated with specific foods. A particular food—for example, a type of fish, fruit, or mushroom—often marks the beginning of its respective season. This, too, is the stuff of news stories and conversation, even at the workplace. In the traditional Japanese home, some of the plates and bowls in which food is served will change with the season—warmer colors during the winter months, lighter colors and the use of glass, suggesting ice, during the hot summer months.

In the belief that Japanese people were working too much, the government in recent years created several new official holidays. There has also been a trend to move the celebration to a Monday nearest to when the holiday occurs, which can sometimes create confusion in scheduling. There are also traditional holidays that are not officially sanctioned as holidays, and while these do not affect work schedules, they are worth noting because they may hold special meaning for some of your coworkers, especially, in many cases, those with young children. It is always good to have a feel for what is happening in the society as a whole, what people are anticipating or doing. Television programs and newspapers, in features and in advertising, often provide clues. Expressing curiosity about traditional occasions for celebrations, such as *Setsubun*, when the ogres of bad luck are sent away and good fortune invited in, or *Shichi-go-san*, for families with children ages seven, five, and three, may provide an opening to conversations with young parents with whom one works and lead to a better understanding of the culture, even though those holidays are not celebrated at work.

FIVE "CALENDARS"

The dates and events that give shape and meaning to the year in Japan, as almost everywhere, derive from a mix of astronomy, history, folklore, religious traditions, institutional decisions, and a bit of astrology, too. In Japan these different ways of marking or experiencing the year are omnipresent and experienced simultaneously; only an outsider might consider these as "five calendars": the Gregorian calendar, the same calendar but with the years calibrated to the reign of each successive emperor, the cultural calendar of seasonal events and days, the calendars of the major institutions (such as "the fiscal year," or "the academic year," and the zodiacal calendar.

The Gregorian or "Western" calendar (*seireki*) is the largely internationally recognized version of how a year is reckoned from Greco-Roman and Christian origins. Japan adopted the Western calendar during the Meiji period (mid-nineteenth century), when so many ideas and innovations from Europe and the Americas were transforming Japanese society. As in the Gregorian calendar, each year begins on January 1 and ends on December 31. This calendar looks very much like the calendar that hangs on walls in Boston and London; the only apparent difference is that the months are named for the number in the twelve-month sequence

There is also the Japanese *gengō* calendar in which, since the Emperor Meiji, each year bears the name of the imperial reign and is numbered in sequence from when that era began. For example, the first year of Emperor Meiji, when Japan dramatically shifted from the centuries of feudal times to the beginning of what became the modern era was in 1868: This is Meiji 1. After the death of the emperor Meiji, the Taisho era began: Taisho 1 is 1912. Showa 1 was 1926; the Showa era spanned more than the six decades that included the pre- and post World War II years and the emergence of Japan as the prominent nation that it is seen as today. The current era, Heisei, began in 1989. Both Western and gengō calendars are used in Japan, but for different purposes. For domestic use, the *gengō* calendar, though seen less often in recent years is still used in many official documents and by many schools, businesses, and other organizations, and there are organizations that use both dating systems.

Apart from these formal numerical calendar systems there is the sense of the year that is given shape by events and seasons, a sense of the year that is the stuff of memory and anticipation to which everyone in Japan is attuned but which may be less apparent to the newcomer. This calendar includes the last day of the year, December 31 (*Ōmisoka*), and the first of the year, January 1 (*Oshōgatsu*), which, in many respects, are the most important days of the year. The end of December is characterized by a flurry of activity of clearing up what can be completed, and cleaning everything—factories, offices, schools, and homes—in preparation for the new year.

This culturally important event calendar includes the time for mid-year gifts (*chūgen*) and those at the end of the year (*seibo*). Traditionally, these gifts are given to those for whom one feels a special social indebtedness for kindnesses given, such as the go-between in a marriage, a child's piano teacher, or the family doctor. These times coincide with and draw upon the two times when, at least until recent years, all bonuses would be paid. This calendar also notes *Obon*, the time when the spirits return and so when many Japanese go back to their *furusato* (parent's hometown) to clean gravesites and honor the deceased in the family. Obon is thus also a time of congested highways and trains, and airlines are fully booked. These and other times of the year are, of course, very much in the Japanese consciousness when making plans, even though the printed calendars at work may not include these dates and events.

For the newcomer in Japan, sensing the special feelings and relative importance of certain dates or times of the year, is often learned through misjudgment. "Why didn't someone tell me?" is a common lament. One former intern felt terrible when he failed to appreciate what it meant when he asked a coworker to help him with a project on the afternoon right before the beginning of Obon. When he later realized that this was right before one of the rare breaks in the year and a time when many families had made special preparations, he said "I realized that it was like I was asking someone at home to help me on Christmas Eve!"

There are also the calendars of companies and organizations which exist in planning and scheduling, and for individuals exists in experience, memories, and expectations. It is in April when the school year begins (from *yōchien*—kindergarten—through the university) and when new employees (*Shinnyūshain*) formally enter companies or other private and public organizations. Identification with one's cohorts, *dōki*, begins then, as does the formation of senior-subordinate relationships and the calculating of seniority. For Western expatriates coming to join a Japanese organization, it is often much easier if one arrives at this time in order to be in sync with the other new regular employees, for there is a whole rhythm of welcoming and orientation events that follows the formal welcome. Some of the busiest times in schools and offices occur just before April, when final preparations are being made for what is very much the beginning of the cycle of a new year.

There is also the *eto* (zodiacal) calendar, which Japan shares with other Asian cultures, the twelve-year cycle of years, each with its animal symbol and attendant qualities. Much as the contemporary Western horoscope associates personality qualities with the month and day of birth, the eto favors the qualities associated with the eto year and totemic animal. Each animal symbol suggests personal qualities for one born that year, with some combinations thought to augur well for marriage partners. Some people anticipate what kind of year it will be according to the year's animal and its ascribed qualities. Each eto year also augurs well or ill for the events that will unfold during its twelve-month presence, though it is not apparent that these associated qualities exert much influence on decisions during the year.

Japanese use a mnemonic to recall the order of the years, so they can know when the snake, rooster, or dog appear, which is useful for interpersonal relations since knowing a person's animal year makes it easy to calculate someone's age without asking. ("Hmm, Mr. Suzuki says he is a *tora* (tiger), so he must have been born in 1986 or 1998—he looks young but he can't be twenty-four so he must be thirty-six.") Telling officemates one's animal year allows others to make a quick calculation of one's age.

DAY BY DAY: THE ALMANAC

Almanacs, which have a strong Chinese influence, became popular in Japan after the Second World War and influence some commercial and social activities. The Japanese government does not pay attention to these auguries, but some businesses do, as do many Japanese. Those days each month identified as *tomobiki* (literally, to pull a friend) are good days for a wedding, but obviously not for a funeral. Some may prefer *taian* (literally, "big lucky day") for a wedding, but the wedding halls may be fully booked on those days.

THE SHAPE OF THE YEAR

Being in sync with the rhythm of the year is essential in Japan. Like any informal feature of a culture, people assume that everyone knows what's happening, and what's expected. What may be most noticed is when something, or someone, is out of sync. There are seasonal events, some formally recognized, as holidays. Other seasonal events are part of the informal culture, and these are even more important.

For one who has come from abroad to work in Japan, nothing feels better than to feel " in sync" with what everyone else is feeling and maybe celebrating. Nothing feels worse than to be out of it. Being in sync lets the communication flow. Missing what is happening is a lost opportunity.

Going to work in Japan means paying attention and being in sync with the holidays and events. Sensing what others are concerned about and dealing with, and being able to express interest and sometimes also a kind of sympathy, is appreciated. As context is a first consideration, being aware of what is happening reflects one's basic respect for others, and for those new to the culture, it can be an opportunity to create or enhance a personal connection that is different and separate from work-related relations.

四 月 *April: The Month of Beginnings*

While formally the year begins in January, historically and institutionally and, for many, emotionally the year begins in the spring. The Japanese academic year starts in April. This is also when the new graduates from college join companies and other private and public organizations. These rites are marked by ceremonies: *Nyūgaku-shiki* (the entrance ceremony for new students) is a very important occasion., *Shin-gakki* is the start of a new semester). Similarly at the company, *Nyūsha-shiki* (the ceremony in which the new employees are welcomed) is also very important. The formal marking of new beginnings is taken very seriously in Japan.

Sakura (cherry blossoms) are also associated with a new beginning, coinciding with the events described above. In April, many people go out to view sakura in the mountains or at public parks and enjoy picnics with family, friends, and coworkers under the sakura. Some companies make it a tradition to enjoy *hanami* parties (cherry blossom viewing parties) at night, and often one of the first assignments for the newly hired is to find and stake out a space at the public park or other popular site selected for the company's party.

五 月 *May: A Month of Holidays and*
Post-Holiday Sickness

The period from the end of April through early May is one of Japan's favorite times of the year. This is called Golden Week, which uses the English words to highlight this succession of days that create Japan's national spring break. Roads will be packed, trains crowded, and airlines fully booked at high rates. The period of Golden Week is more important than the particular starring holiday in this constellation. There is *Shōwa no hi* (birthday of the emperor Showa, April 29, followed by *Kenpō kinen-bi* (Constitution Day) on May 3; *Midori no hi* (Green Day, one of the newer holidays inserted to maintain a sequence of holidays, and established to celebrate the earth and promote a healthy ecology) is May 4. May 5 is *Tango no sekku* or *Kodomo no hi* (Children's Day). It is for this day that all over Japan those colorful cloth "flying carp" (*koi nobori*) are seen streaming in the wind atop of pole. Children's Day traditionally celebrated boys but now it is intended to honor all children (though the symbolism one sees mostly centers on boys).

Depending on the policy of the company or school, and also depending on how weekends fall in new year, it is possible to have a holiday break that lasts a week or even longer.

After the excitement of joining the company or other organization, the new environment and starting to know new people, and having that Golden Week break, some people in Japan show symptoms of emotional and even physical distress: loss of interest, motivation, and actual physical fatigue. After the excitement, it is now back to work with no more holidays until late July. Some will suffer from *Gogatsu-byō* (May sickness).

六月　*June: A Time of Rain and, for Many, a Time for a Bonus in the Paycheck*

With not even one holiday this month, June is mostly known for *tsuyu* (the rainy season). It is also bonus season. Depending on the company, the end of June or sometimes early July is the time when employees may receive their semiannual bonus. In a stable economy the amount of the bonus has been anticipated by the recipient and figured into the household budget, so while this is the awaited good news, it is not a bonus to be splurged. This is not party time; more likely it is dentist, piano, or tuition savings time.

By the end of June, beginning in the south and moving north, the tsuyu season is over, but the typhoon season begins, affecting Okinawa first and reaching "the mainland" of Japan later, with its might to be expected in August and the weeks that follow.

七月　*July: As School Closes, the Sea and the Mountains are Now Open*

July is when the sun breaks out and the first part of the school year comes to an end.

Most schools have closing ceremonies for the first semester and a brief summer vacation begins. *Umi no hi* (Ocean Day), another relatively new national holiday, is July 20. Around this time the beaches open (*umibiraki*). This time of year, with school vacation and some company vacations, travel costs increase, especially for international travel. Airline fees can double.

八月　*August: Natsu-yasumi: Summer Vacation*

August is the time of *Obon*, when many people return to their hometown (*furusato*) or historic family place. Obon is the day which tradition says the spirits of one's ancestors come back to their homeland. For expatriates in Japan, *Obon* may be known as another holiday time, and when there are beautiful summer events including dances in the evening that evoke a Japan of the past. For many

Japanese, however, this is a spiritual time of receiving and hosting the spirits of those in the family that have departed and visit again so briefly. The rivers and ocean carry the spirits into the land and back to the sea. For this reason, too, the summer's swimming season ends with Obon, lest the spirits invite and then pull the innocent under the water.

Summer is vacation time (*natsu-yasumi*) for children and college students and, for a few days, for employees, many of whom enjoy some paid vacations as well. This is also when many summer festivals (*natsu-matsuri*) are held and most businesses close around August 13 through August 15.

九 月 *September: Back to Work*

Summer vacation ends, the work pace picks up at the company and students return to school in September for the second semester (*nigakki/kōki*). *Keirō no hi* (Respect for Elders Day) is celebrated in mid-September), and *Shun-bun no hi* (Autumn Equinox Day) is September 23. Around the third week of September this series of consecutive holidays is called Silver Week.

Also around this time, depending on when in the lunar calendar the full moon appears, families and friends may enjoy *Otsukimi*, the night to view autumn's full moon.

十 月 *October: A Time of Good Weather, School Festivals, and Sports Activities*

With good autumn weather, this is the season for outdoor activities. Around the second week of October is *Taiku no hi* (Sports Day), a national holiday. Many school sporting events are scheduled for this time of the year. (It is a good time to ask coworkers who have children in school about these events, for they may be much involved with their children's events. (If you are invited to visit, do not decline.)

The *kōyo* (autumn leaves) season begins in mid-October and extends well into November. Japan's renowned autumn foliage, especially maple leaves (*momiji*), attract millions of people to the temples, shrines, parks, and mountains.

十 一 月 *November: Autumn Leaves*

November brings beautiful weather in most of Japan and is a busy time at the office. Officially there is *Bunka no hi* (Culture Day), which is a time for weekend school festivals that attract parents, alumni, and townspeople.

十二月 *December: Farewell to the Year: Bōnen-kai*

December is one of the busiest months of the year, with some holidays and many activities in companies and schools as the official year comes to a close. December 23 is a national holiday for the emperor's birthday (*Tennō tanjō-bi*), which is also when winter vacation begins for most schools, and so a day when many employees will be adjusting at home. December is also the other semiannual bonus time.

December 24 and 25, Christmas Eve and Christmas, have no religious significance for most Japanese (only about 1 percent of Japanese identify themselves as Christian), but these days are increasingly a part of the social and commercial scene in Japan, and feature many of the familiar Western symbols of the season. Christmas Eve also holds a romantic appeal for young couples, much like Valentine's Day elsewhere—restaurants and hotels are booked by young romantic couples.

Toshinose (the end of the year) is a time of great activity at work and after hours with friends and colleagues, the time for year-end parties, *bōnen-kai* (literally, a gathering to forget the past year), which are among the liveliest of the year.

Around December 28 and 29, the last days of work are called *shigoto-osame* (finishing the job for the year). Many companies make this last workday of the year a day for all employees to clean the office, even the windows, to make a new start with a clean workplace for the new year. A part of the continuity that goes back to the *yōchien*.

December 31, New Year's Eve (*Ōmisoka*), is the last of the busiest times and when Japanese prepare for the New Year holiday. Traditionally people used to prepare all their New Year's holiday meals by the end of the year, so that they would not need to spend time in the kitchen for the first days of the new year. This is also the time to clean the entire home. On Ōmisoka temples bells are rung 108 times (*joya no kane*), finishing before midnight. The shrines and temples throughout Japan are packed with visitors enjoying the busy scene, with holiday vendors offering festival foods and sometimes entertainment. Those who don't venture out will watch the temple and entertainment events on television.

一月 *January: New Year's Ritual Events, Socializing, and New Beginnings at Work*

Koto hajime: everything begins anew. The advent. The new year that begins after the flurry of activity in December and the quiet and imagining of a good beginning of the new year. Many Japanese express this special time with visits to shrines or maybe (mostly) watching television to see others at some of the most famous sites.

January first, second, and third are national holidays. January 1 (*Oshōgatsu*), especially, is a day for families to relax and enjoy special New Year's Days' foods, including foods which use ingredients that symbolize good health, long life, and prosperity. The holiday would be incomplete without these foods, including *osechi-ryōri* and *mochi*), whether prepared at home or, increasingly, purchased ready-made. Traditionally almost all stores, including department stores and supermarkets, were closed for at least these three days, or even for a full week, but now many stores open even on January first, offering the year's "first sales." During these first days, most transportation follows a holiday schedule, with fewer buses and trains.

After the first three days of the new year, yet still officially part of the New Year's days celebrations, comes *shigoto-hajime*, the occasion to formally mark the first day of work, usually on January 4. On this day, many companies meet for a few hours to formally offer their New Year's greeting and welcome anew everyone in the company. Many women, especially those who work at banks or at investment firms, attend in traditional kimono. This day, or evening, may also be a time for people to get together for a *shinnen-kai* (a party to celebrate the new year). The actual first day of work begins the following day.

Traditionally January 15, but now the second Monday in January, is a national holiday to celebrate people who turn twenty this year (*Seijin no hi*), with ceremonies at city halls and municipal government buildings. Many young people dress in traditional clothing. Age twenty also is the legal drinking age and the age when one is eligible to vote.

Starting at the end of January and sometimes extending as late as March is when universities, high schools, and junior high schools conduct their entrance exams (*nyūgaku-shiken*). These are intense, stressful times for prospective students and their families, and schools are very busy preparing for the testing. Even for those not involved, there is sympathy shaped by memories of perhaps the most emotional, stressful time in one's life.

二 月 *February: The Coldest Month and a Quiet Time at Schools and Companies*

Setsubun is not a national holiday, but it's a favorite day when the tossing of parched beans invites good luck in and throws out bad luck. Like some of the other holidays, this day has no significance whatsoever at work, but for coworkers with young children it may be a special day and thus an opportunity to inquire and engage in a new conversation.

Kenkoku kinen-bi (Foundation Day), February 11, is a national holiday that celebrates, according to Japanese mythology, the day Japan was founded.

Usually February is the coldest month throughout Japan, and a time of snow festivals (*Yuki-matsuri*) in Japan's "snow country." The festival in Sapporo, with its elaborate snow sculptures, is the best known internationally.

三月 *March: The Event Calendar Comes Full Circle*

Sotsugyō-shiki (graduation ceremonies) take place in March, with the newly graduated anticipating entering the workforce the following month. For most businesses this is the end of the fiscal year, and therefore it is also the busiest season for many.

While not a national holiday, March 3, Girls' Day, (*Hina-matsuri*), is a favorite day of celebration, when young girls are honored and a traditional set of princess and royal court dolls (*hina-ningyō*) are displayed, and traditional foods are served to the daughters and their friends. Like other holidays, the displays of the court in store windows and, often elaborately, at hotels and other public places, make this a holiday hard to overlook. Like other holidays it is an occasion through which to express interest in and, in the process, to become more in sync with the season.

✝

TEN

Going to Work in Japan: Seven Suggestions

In the list of fifty years of research findings regarding cultural adjustment, and "culture shock," one anchor in the sea of confusion is a "tolerance of ambiguity," being okay with not quite understanding everything that is going on around one. Ambiguity, inconsistency, contraction . . . these are features of cultures everywhere, not the least our own. An important part of our enculturation as we grow up is learning to get along with a personal world that upon closer examination seems not at all "consistent." While finding patterns that suddenly help make sense of our new experiences is very important, tolerating the inability to understand those, or allowing that those inconsistencies are part of where we are, is also a quality advised. In some contexts and with some important friendships we can explore the real or apparent inconsistencies and learn from the discussion. The "war stories" that expats everywhere tell about "what's wrong with these people" only strengthen the intolerance and prevent a cultural understanding.

If you were just beginning to work in Japan and had a chance to talk with someone who was once in a similar situation, you might ask if the person had any advice to share. In this chapter we offer seven suggestions.

REMEMBER WHY YOU WERE
FIRST INTERESTED IN JAPAN

Most of the people interviewed in our research were initially attracted to Japan for reasons unrelated to their work. The attraction to Japan was more likely to be manga or martial arts than a desire to work at an office or lab. It was later that the interest in doing serious work in Japan developed, but many who seemed most satisfied with their experience spoke of how important it was to also reconnect with those earlier interests.

Do not ignore personal interests that may have nothing to do with Japan in particular, for they provide a point of connection, and the cultural differences which become apparent are usually a source of curiosity and often delight when they are not the focus. In Japan one can find organizations, events, classes, and clubs devoted to every kind of interest. If you play a musical instrument, there will be a band or even an orchestra you can join. If you were active in sports, there is probably a team—sometimes as part of the company—you can join.

Though most Japanese have a special pride in their history, art, technology and more, and an appreciation for those from abroad who want to learn more about their culture on a visit, expats who make Japan their home may be puzzling. Professor Richard Harris, a transplanted Londoner who has lived for three decades in Nagoya, remarks:

> Talking with Japanese friends here, I think that there is often a general incomprehension as to why so many expats would want to leave their homes and come here at all. The sense of 'belonging' is much more powerful than the sense of "adventure" or "wanting to live abroad for the experience" that motivates so many [to come to Japan], and yet is only dimly understood, if at all, by many Japanese. . . . Of course most ex-pats are made extremely welcome in Japan and are treated with great generosity and kindness. Gone are the days when children burst into tears (or laughter) at the sight of *gaijin*; respectful curiosity is more of a norm.

There are practical reasons for pursuing personal interests, reasons that extend beyond the personal. In the context of the office or laboratory, roles and relationships are near the surface. There are pressures arising from a project and a self-consciousness of meeting expectations of supervisors and coworkers. One will learn, often a great deal, but it will be different from what is acquired in a more social, less pressured-setting and one feels that less is at stake. Ironically, but consistent with what is known about acculturation, one may learn faster and more easily away from work than at work. Nobel Prize winning physicist and author Richard Feynman wrote that he often learned more from hanging out at "seedy bars" (his words) off-campus while at Princeton than with colleagues. He was alluding to the value of being with people whose worlds are different from the familiar professional world of friends and colleagues. Japan has no shortage of seedy bars, but that is not the suggestion. Rather, the advice is to take seriously your interests with other serious people outside of work.

KEEP WORKING ON YOUR JAPANESE

It was nearly unanimous among those interviewed who had worked in Japan for six months or more that continuing to work on learning Japanese was crucial. Whether in formal classes, sometimes offered right where one is working, or in informal conversation gatherings in the community, there are always opportunities to improve one's Japanese. That liminal time between when the official work day is over and before people actually leave work can offer a chance to do some studying, and in that context it is also a tacit indication of one's seriousness, and may show an openness for others to offer their encouragement and help.

Insecurity about language ability is normal, and rationalizations about not doing more to learn ("I won't be here all that long," or "I'm sure I can just pick it up on my own") are usually self-defeating and can produce feelings of regret that last longer than the time in Japan.

ENGLISH SPOKEN HERE

A few of the people we interviewed expressed regret that they missed opportunities to connect with others in the office because they felt that some of their coworkers seemed mostly interested in practicing their English. A few people reported being frustrated that their role in the company seemed to be limited to their English language ability rather than their competence professionally, but providing assistance in English (or another foreign language) is often a part of the western expat's expected role, as in reviewing correspondence in English or helping with translations. Others said that they avoided those at the office who seemed to want to practice their English while the expat wanted to concentrate on Japanese. It is not an either-or situation but some, like this person, experienced it that way and then later saw it as a missed opportunity to form friendships.

"My biggest regret" was that I was so selfish as to try to avoid those moments when it was obvious that the other person wanted to practice English. I was thinking, "Well, I am in Japan—don't expect me to speak English." But now I realize that from point of view of my coworker it was probably, "Here is someone from the U.S. It's a rare chance to speak English with someone in the office." "I feel bad for what must have disappointed people there. Now I imagine that the manager may have encouraged everyone to welcome me in part because they could practice their English. But worse, I missed so many chances to give what little I could to that office, times to speak in English. It was selfish of me, and a missed opportunity to get to know some of my coworkers and to learn from them as well."

TALK ABOUT FOOD

"What do you miss?" is a question commonly asked of friends who have returned home from living abroad. When those who have lived in Japan are asked, "the food" is usually one of the first things that is mentioned. The number of food and food-related words that have come into Western languages recently is a clear indicator: sushi, ramen, wasabi, o-bento. Japan is a nation which both exudes a sense of national culture ("we Japanese") and sensitivity to regional variations in history, dialect, and especially in food. When most people traveled by trains slower than the Shinkan-sen, it was a feature of travel to decide which stop en route to choose the particular kind of food offered in the station bento. Food obtained from a particular region is the preferred gift for vacationers to share with officemates and friends. Airports and train stations stock foods from all parts of Japan so that the traveler who forgot to pick up something for a friend could still get something when returning and not have that lapse in thoughtfulness be obvious.

British anthropologist Gregory Bateson has remarked that "food is love," and there is truth in that equation. If you like me, you will like my food; the converse is even more obvious—if you don't enjoy my food, then you must not like my people and me.

In Japan, there are times and ways to express interest in and appreciation for local food as in few other places in the world. Even within a city, there are varieties of each kind of food, and each with its own history and the pride that sustains it. For those who come to work and live in Japan, the subject of food offers one of the best points of engagement and to express curiosity and appreciation, a time to learn so much and to make a personal connection.

"I NOTICED ON TELEVISION . . ."

For generations, Westerners have associated Japan with the aesthetics of gardens, architecture, pottery, all forms of design, and classic films. Today Japan is known even more through mass media and many aspects of its "popular culture." ("Hello Kitty" who first appeared in 1975 now is seen more often and in more places than Mickey Mouse.) Animation filmmaker Hayao Miyazaki may be more famous internationally today than legendary directors like Kurosawa and Ozu. Manga and anime are not only terms borrowed into English and subjects of graduate study at universities throughout the world, they have also influenced children's drawings and adult fashion. Wacky Japanese game shows are seen by millions on YouTube all over the world.

Even if none of Japan's popular culture extended beyond its shores, anyone who goes to work in Japan is advised to give a little attention to the latest fad—there is always at least one. Note how the locals' favorite baseball team is doing. Become aware of popular singers, actors, and even "teenage idols" whose images are everywhere. Though most may not be taken too seriously, showing an awareness of what is going on outside of the workplace conveys a message in itself, and it can lead to more conversations that are much more interesting than talking about the weather.

KEEP A JOURNAL

Some people make it a habit to keep a journal, and others have never felt any need or interest to record their experiences and reflections. Many more people send, and often retain a record of, e-mail messages to friends and family. Some people blog. A record of e-mails (and blogs) can serve as a kind of journal without additional effort. There is a difference, however, in what we might tell ourselves in a journal and what we might tell others, and so one suggestion is to write e-mails to oneself, too, and keep these as a record. In addition to serving some small historical purpose, a review of some of the experience can serve as a personal report on things that were first confusing but later seemed less so. And, things that seemed simple or obvious sometimes turn out to be far more complex and merit further consideration. The journal can also serve as a reminder of questions and interests to pursue that sometimes become lost or forgotten when one is busy every day. People you meet whom you would like to get to know better, a recommendation of an event to take in or a place to visit, and many other matters that you intend to follow up on: much that is happening in a new environment may be best noted in a journal, whatever its form.

MAKE A FRIEND

This last suggestion may seem the simplest, though there may be times when it might feel like the most difficult. It is the advice most often given by Edward T. Hall, who is generally regarded as launching the contemporary exploration of intercultural communication. Get to know someone from Japan whom you enjoy being with, irrespective of your professional work. In Hall's terms, "Make a friend." You can learn more from talking with your friend about more things that matter, about living and working in Japan and about communication in Japan, than through any other source. Not technical or specialized information needed at work, but about communication and relationships, which are even more important.

APPENDIX

Some Useful Terms to Know When Going to Work in Japan

MEETINGS

- *Chōrei* (morning orientation). Some companies might have chōrei every morning, while others might hold it every Monday. Employees in a division or a larger section may get together and have a short meeting for general announcements.
- *Kaigi* (a formal meeting). Japanese kaigi are famous for lasting many hours. A *jūyaku kaigi* is an executive meeting.
- *Mītingu* (meeting). Japanese have borrowed the word from English. The word may be used interchangeably for *kaigi* or *uchiawase*; mītingu sounds more informal than kaigi.
- *Uchiawase.* This type of meeting is for practical scheduling or for information sharing. This can be used both for meetings within a company and with business partners.

TITLES AND RELATIONSHIPS

- *Shachō*. President of a company.
- *Buchō*. Director of a department.
- *Kachō*. Chief of a division.
- *Kakarichō*. Chief of a section.
- *Shinnyū-shain/Shinjin*. Newly hired employees, usually those who have just graduated from school.
- *Jōshi* and *buka*. Jōshi is a supervisor; buka is a subordinate.
- *Senpai* and *kōhai*. In the work context, a senpai is a person who entered a company before you and/or has more experience; kōhai is a person who joined a company after you and is usually younger than you.
- *Dōkisei/dōki*. In the work context, employees who start at the same company at the same time.
- *Torihiki-saki*. Other companies that do business with your company. Sometimes such a company may be called *Torihikisaki-san*, just as if it were a person.

TYPES OF WORKERS

- *Shain*. Company's employee.
- *Sei-shain*. Full-time employees. Traditionally, sei-shain status in Japan meant "life-time employment."
- *Keiyaku-shain*. Contract workers. Part-time workers may be included in this category. Keiyaku-shain are hired directly by a company or sent by a personnel service company. Their salaries are paid on an hourly basis and their insurance or compensation packages are different from those of full-time workers.
- *Kenshū-sei*. Interns. In Japanese organizations, even if kenshū-sei are hired for full-time positions, the first several months are a "trial time." Therefore, they may be called kenshū-sei or *shinnyū-shain/ shinjin* (new employees).
- *Arubaito* (*Albait*) Part-time workers. Albait are similar to keiyaku-shain, as their salaries are paid on an hourly basis. However, albait arrangements are less stable and usually indicate more of a temporary position. Part-time jobs for college students are in this category.
- *Frītā* (*Freeter*) Part-time workers. This word appeared in the 1990s when young college graduates could not find full-time employment due to the economic recession. Around the same time Japan began to see young people

who chose not to commit themselves to long-term employment. Both by force of circumstance and also by choice, people who take albait work and for a variety of reasons move from one job to another are identified by this term.

- *O.L.* Office ladies.

PARTIES AT WORK

- *Kangei-kai.* Welcoming party.
- *Sōbetsu-kai.* Farewell party.
- *Bōnen-kai.* The end of year party.
- *Shinnen-kai.* New Year's party.

ADDITIONAL RESOURCES

There are so many resources on Japan available today in English, publications and a niagara of information and commentary flowing through the internet each day, that it is difficult to select just a few things to recommend. However, here are two suggestions. If you have some hobby or special interest in a subject, look for books on that subject as it relates to Japan—anime, music, theater, sports, whatever. Any good bookstore that features books on and/or from Japan will have titles to intrigue and delight. Often the best route to understanding a culture is by way of some personal interest, particularly one that can be developed and discussed with Japanese friends and colleagues at work. A Japanese executive who lived in the United States for many years recommends that in addition to reading books on Japan that are intended primarily for foreigners, it is also important to read what the Japanese themselves are reading. This will give you something of mutual interest that can be discussed. These include books written by popular Japanese authors that have been translated into English. Do not overlook works of fiction. Haruki Murakami's novels, for example, are widely available in English and other translations. His short stories also frequently appear in *The New Yorker*. Similarly, books that are originally in English (or other Western languages) are likely to be published in Japanese translation; indeed, sometimes the Japanese translations outsell the book in its original form. The Japanese press, including in its English language editions, provides up-to-date best-sellers reports.

For keeping up on what is happening, there are four daily newspapers published in Japan in English—more than in any city in the U.S. today. These are the *Asahi*, the *Mainichi*, the *Yomiuri*, and *The Japan Times*, which is the largest of the English language papers. Each has not only Japanese and international news, but also news features, columns, and translations from items in the Japanese press. There are also many specialized and professional journals that publish English language translations of recent Japanese articles. Of particular interest to many of those who go to work in Japan is the *Nihon Keizai Shimbun* (with an English language weekly, the *Nikkei Weekly*); there are also news items and commentary in English available online.

We also encourage browsing at one of the large Japanese bookstores such as Maruzen and the largest, Kinokuniya, which has stores throughout Japan and more than twenty stores overseas, including eight in the United States. It is reported that in Australia, the Kinokuniya bookstore is the largest bookstore. In these stores in Japan one will discover a remarkably wide selection of books on Japan in English and other Western languages, and one can also observe what the Japanese readers are interested in today.

Finally we should note that Intercultural Press, the publisher of this book, offers a number of fine books to consider. Among those that may be most relevant to topics considered in this book are *The New Japan* by David Matsumoto; *The Art of Crossing Cultures*, Second Edition, by Craig Storti; *Hidden Differences: Doing Business with the Japanese* by Edward T. Hall and Mildred Reed Hall; and *A Beginner's Guide to the Deep Cultural Experience* by Joseph Shaules.

INDEX

CROSSING CULTURES

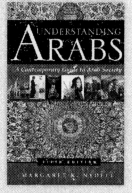

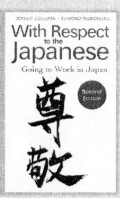

**AMONG THE
IRANIANS**
*A Guide to Iran's
Culture and Customs*
by Sofia A. Koutlaki
ISBN: 9781931930901
E-ISBN: 9780984247134
US Price: $24.95
UK Price: £14.99

**AU CONTRAIRE!
SECOND ED.**
Figuring Out the French
by Gilles Asselin and
Ruth Mastron
ISBN: 9781931930925
E-ISBN: 9780984247189
US Price: $29.95
UK Price: £16.99

**ENCOUNTERING
THE CHINESE,
THIRD ED.**
*A Modern Country, An
Ancient Culture*
by Hu Wenzhong,
Cornelius N. Grove, and
Zhuang Enping
ISBN: 9781931930994
E-ISBN: 9780984247196
US Price: $24.95
UK Price: £14.99

**FROM NYET TO DA,
FOURTH ED.**
*Understanding the New
Russia*
by Yale Richmond
ISBN: 9781931930598
E-ISBN: 9781931930727
US Price: $27.95
UK Price: £14.99

GERMANY
Unraveling An Enigma
by Greg Nees
ISBN: 9781877864759
E-ISBN: 9781931930420
US Price: $27.50
UK Price: £12.99

**LEARNING TO
THINK KOREAN**
*A Guide to Living and
Working in Korea*
by L. Robert Kohls
ISBN: 9781877864872
E-ISBN: 9781931930437
US Price: $35.00
UK Price: £16.99

**MODERN-DAY
VIKINGS**
*A Practical Guide to
Interacting with the Swedes*
by Christina Johansson
Robinowitz and Lisa
Werner Carr
ISBN: 9781877864889
E-ISBN: 9780585434414
US Price: $25.95
UK Price: £16.99

**SPAIN IS DIFFERENT,
SECOND ED.**
by Helen Wattley-Ames
ISBN: 9781877864711
E-ISBN: 9781931930819
US Price: $19.95
UK Price: £10.99